D1243829

ISBN 978-1-943521-52-4

Boyack, Connor, author.
Stanfield, Elijah, illustrator.
Weber, Brenden, editor.
The Tuttle Twins Guide to Logical Fallacies / Connor Boyack.

Cover design by Elijah Stanfield
Edited and typeset by Connor Boyack

Printed in the United States

10 9 8 7 6 5 4 3 2 1

THE TUTTLE TWINS GUIDE TO
LOGICAL FALLACIES

BY CONNOR BOYACK

The List of
FALLACIES

Hey there! We're the Tuttle Twins, and you're holding a dangerous book.

Well, it's not dangerous for you. It's dangerous for the people you interact with: your parents, siblings, teachers, neighbors, and friends.

Why? Because this book is going to make you better at thinking and debating. You're going to be more effective at persuading other people, and you're going to poke holes in the incorrect arguments made by others.

But remember, with great power comes great responsibility. It's up to you to use this information the right way.

Here's the thing: as we've grown up, our parents and friends have been teaching us all sorts of things about the way the world works and the problems that happen when some people try to control others.

We've been involved in starting small businesses, changing laws, doing some fun marketing projects, and more. But along the way, we realized that many people don't know how to argue well.

Let's clear something up, though. We're

not talking about being *argumentative*. We're talking about forming good arguments so that as you learn important and true things, you can teach them to others.

Along the way, you're going to encounter lots of bad ideas. Looooots of them. The world is full of them. They're taught in schools, and they're all over the Internet. They are touted by celebrities and turned into catchy tunes.

As you learn true principles and correct data, it's going to be helpful to know how to defend them from others who may try to attack your point of view. You'll also want to know how to point out someone else's poor logic that doesn't support their point of view. Again, not to be argumentative, but to form good arguments.

We're here as your guide as you learn about all the (many!) logical fallacies that people use—errors in reasoning that make an argument invalid. We'll pop up throughout the book to share some examples.

Again, this is dangerous stuff. If you really try to understand the ideas in this book, you're going to be a force to be reckoned with among your family and friends. Use your power wisely!

—The Tuttle Twins

The
STRAWMAN

In order to avoid debating the real issue, an opponent misrepresents your argument by creating a counterfeit one that is easier to refute, and then they declare themselves the victor.

Beware the Strawman!

When you're presented with a strong argument against an idea you believe in, it may be difficult to face it head on. Chances are, it will require research and thought, but if you're in a conversation or argument, you don't have a lot of time on your hands. You have to think quickly and have a rebuttal ready, or simply say "I don't know," which is hard for many people to do.

Enter the temptation of the strawman. Imagine living on a farm and creating your own man of straw. You can make him look like your worst enemy if you wanted to; you can be creative in customizing the straw creature in front of you. Perhaps to add a little flair, you give him horns, an ugly scowl, and weak limbs. Now the fun part: imagine lighting that strawman on fire to defeat your enemy. Would it feel good? Would it feel like you were actually harming your enemy?

Problem is, of course, it's not a real person. It's a creation of your own making, and it doesn't address the problems you have with that other person; it doesn't resolve the actual conflict between you and the other person.

Now instead of creating a fake enemy, imagine creating a fake argument. You can attack that newly concocted argument and have a convincing way to show how wrong it is. Maybe you come up with a clever story or think up a fact that proves it wrong.

Problem is, of course, you haven't addressed the other person's actual argument. You've instead responded to a creation of your own making, much like the strawman. It may feel good, but it hasn't resolved anything. The person's argument hasn't been undermined in any way.

If anything, you've weakened your own position by spending time and energy on an argument that your opponent didn't make. And when the person points it out to others who may be watching, listening to, or reading your conversation, he'll gain the upper hand and look smarter. Then others might be more inclined to believe him, because when given the opportunity to address his argument, you didn't, and perhaps couldn't.

So you need to address the argument head on, just as you should resolve conflict with another person rather than lighting fake straw people on fire. (Seriously, who does that?) What you need to fight here is the temptation to burn your enemy, rather than his argument. In an emotional debate—let's say, over whether your family member in the military is helping or hurting people in another country—it can be very tempting to oppose the person rather than his or her arguments.

This is especially true in political debates where each faction or team is rooting for "their guy" and is willing to win at all costs. Scoring a victory in a debate is the goal, so attacking the person is considered acceptable, as is distorting what he's actually saying. Defeating the enemy becomes as valuable as (if not more so than) defeating his arguments.

That's a bad idea, and it's why politics is so toxic—the goal is victory in an election, rather than the defense of a good idea. So for those of us who care about ideas—and values and principles and truth—*we have to make sure not to resort to the same tactics as those who don't.* That means learning to identify and fight the strawman fallacy. It is used quite often, so you need to practice recognizing it and avoid falling prey to it.

The use of a strawman argument usually consists of the following three parts:

- Person A states their position.

- Person B presents a distorted version of Person A's original position, while pretending that there's no difference between the two versions.

- Person B attacks the distorted version of Person A's position, and acts as if this invalidates Person A's original argument.

An Example with Ethan and Emily

"I don't get why Josie won't hang out with us anymore," Emily sighed as she slammed the door shut behind her.

Ethan thought he knew the reason why, and his name was Dexter.

When Dexter had moved into the neighborhood earlier in the year, it changed everything. Ethan and Emily were once friends with most of the kids on the block, but now their friends were split. Including Josie.

"She can't stand Dexter," Ethan explained. "And she and her friends don't like hanging out around us when we're with him."

After talking with their parents about what to do, the twins decided the best approach would be to kindly confront Josie and give her the opportunity to explain. They saw her at the tennis court the next morning and approached her to talk.

"Josie, is there a reason you aren't hanging out with us as much as you used to?" Emily asked, tossing her a tennis ball. "We'd like to know what's up."

"You've made your choice, it seems," Josie replied rather firmly. "You want to be friends with that goofball Dexter? Fine. Then I'm going to hang out with other people."

Josie ran off with her racket in hand, leaving Ethan and Emily alone to figure out what had just happened.

What Happened?

First off, it's important to note that Josie was interpreting the thoughts of Ethan and Emily. They never had told Josie they wanted to spend less time with her, or that they valued their friendship with Dexter more than their friendship with her. So the "stated position" was merely an action in this case.

And Josie formed a distorted version of the twins' position. Josie apparently thought that by spending time with Dexter, Ethan and Emily wanted to be friends with him instead of with her. She didn't like that, so she attacked that position by avoiding them altogether.

Josie wasn't resolving a real problem; she was misinterpreting something and reacting to it. This is common with the strawman fallacy. For example, imagine having an aunt who nearly died from cancer, but who benefitted from using cannabis as a medicine. So at a family event, you suggest that the states that prohibit cannabis should let sick people use it if it could help them. A relative who disagrees with that interjects to say how irresponsible you are for wanting more teens to abuse this drug and for more people to drive while intoxicated, creating a danger for everybody on the road.

Of course, you don't support drug abuse or driving while under the influence of drugs, right? That wasn't your point, and you likely would argue that there's a way to allow sick people to get the treatment they need while preventing this parade of horrible things from happening. But your initial point was misrepresented and attacked. It doesn't feel good to be at the receiving end of this one, so make sure you're not using it on others!

Tuttle Twins Takeaway

Don't make a claim about what you *think* a person believes, and then attack them for it. Learn to separate a person from the ideas he believes in, and don't attack or assume something about another. After all, we are each learning and progressing. If you discuss actual ideas, and make sure you correctly understand and debate the ideas another personal actually believes, you can help people abandon bad ones and adopt good ones, without them feeling like you're a slimy jerk just looking to win a debate to impress others.

FALSE CAUSE
Post Hoc Ergo Propter Hoc

Someone will take a relationship between two things and try to argue that one of the things *caused* the other thing, but sometimes this relationship is merely coincidental.

This is the glove I wore when my team beat the Cougars. So now I wear it every game. That's why we keep winning.

It's magic.

On average, the global climate has been rising since the dawn of the industrial age. Clearly human industrial activity is causing this rise in temperature.

Statistically, female employees get paid less than males. This is obviously a result of systematic gender prejudice in business, dude.

Very Superstitious

You've likely encountered a friend who has believed in some sort of superstition about a routine they do before something they care about. Maybe your friend on the cross country team sleeps with their socks on the night before a big race. Another friend might flush an ice cube down the toilet on snowy nights to "increase the chances" of cancelled school for a snow day. Another may wear their "lucky" shoes for a debate tournament!

You might even have a superstition of your own, where you perceive a relationship between an action or routine and some sort of external event. Imagine your friend Tommy who tries to watch every single LeBron James basketball game on TV. As a superstitious ritual, Tommy always tries to wear his LeBron jersey while the game is on, because every time he's remembered to wear the jersey, LeBron's team has won.

Tommy has wrongfully assumed that LeBron winning and him wearing the jersey are somehow connected, and that by wearing his jersey, he has *caused* LeBron to win. He failed to take into account the obvious possibility of coincidence, and instead has happily provided you with an example of the *false cause fallacy*.

This fallacy simply assumes that one thing would not occur without the other. In the case of Tommy, he assumes that not wearing his jersey will result in LeBron losing. The fallacy also occurs in less extreme coincidences in everyday life. Consider the case of Anna who is a server at a restaurant. She claims that when she wears her hair in a bun, customers leave her higher tips than when she wears her hair in a braid. This must mean, according to her, that the way she wears her hair is the reason for her higher tips.

Although the facts of her tip amounts and hair styles may be true, it does not mean that the relationship is directly related. This would be very difficult to prove and is just an assumption based on an observation Anna has noticed without evidence. She fails to consider other factors such as if they were satisfied with their food, or how timely their service was, which has nothing to do with how Anna wears her hair. For all we know, Anna gets hot and therefore cranky when her hair is down, contributing to a poor customer experience!

The false cause fallacy lacks substance for providing reasoning for a claim. If your opponent were to use this tactic, they would have merely pointed out that two events occurred around the same time. Remember, casual connections are hard to establish in argumentation and you must provide reasoning for why they are connected. Pointing out one event happened after another as reasoning is not enough to establish this causal connection!

It is important to learn this fallacy to help you demonstrate proper correlation and causation during a debate with an opponent, so you will not only be able to point out faulty reasoning in others but also determine when two events truly have a connection.

The false cause fallacy is usually presented with two parts:

- Person A says event X is related to or happened after event Y.

- Person A concludes that event X caused event Y.

An Example with Ethan and Emily

It was a cold winter night at their family's cabin. The twins were hanging out with their friend Ashley after a fun day of skiing during their winter break from school.

"Today was so fun! I can't wait for tomorrow," Ethan proclaimed.

"Yeah, I agree! I just hope it snows tonight so we can have some fresh snow for skiing tomorrow," Emily said, looking at Ethan and Ashley.

After a pause in the conversation, as though the three of them were thinking of some way to will some snow into existence, Ashley had an idea.

"Oh! I know exactly what to do to make sure we get snow tonight!"

"What is it? Because I don't know how we can possibly do anything to make snow occur, except maybe pray for it," Ethan replied with skepticism and doubt.

"I have to agree with Ethan on this one, Ashley," Emily added.

Ashley faced them and replied, "Well, there's this ritual I do every time I want it to snow, and every time I remember, it works!"

Ashley gestured to the twins as though she was about to present them with a groundbreaking discovery.

"See, before going to bed I drop an ice cube down the toilet and wear socks to bed," Ashley explained.

"Um, that's your grand scheme to make it snow?" Emily asked with a curious, yet concerned, expression toward Ashley's plan.

Ashley confidently responded, "Yes, I'm letting good ol' Mother Nature know that I'm ready to be blessed with some snow!"

The twins and Ashley went to bed shortly after this discussion. That night it did snow and the next day Ethan and Emily were left to wonder what happened.

What Happened?

The twins' friend Ashley fell for a superstition! She had convinced herself that putting an ice cube down the toilet and wearing socks to bed would bring snowfall that night. But is there any evidence to prove that this ritual is what caused the snowfall?

No. Merely saying her ritual will work and then the event happening hasn't actually proven her claim to be true. For one, this goes against our basic understanding of the weather. Second, as was discussed earlier, just because the snowfall happened to occur after Ashley did her snowfall ritual doesn't actually provide any evidence that the ritual worked. This chain of events is not enough to establish a cause-and-effect connection between the two events. She has wrongly attributed cause and effect to the two events and has wrong argued using a false cause.

To avoid using this fallacy you must learn to properly establish the cause and effect relationship of two events if you are going to offer it as reasoning for your claim.

Ashley confused coincidence with causation. What likely occurred is her ritual was done when she heard about a chance of snow. She decided to perform the ritual after information of snowfall already being possible was presented to her. In this situation her ritual came after an indication that snowfall is possible or likely to occur; her ritual wasn't the cause.

Imagine you are in a conversation with your Uncle Mike. He claims that every time a Republican becomes president the economy gets much worse; therefore, Republican presidents are bad for the economy. For one, to some extent, this can be a coincidence. Second, Mike would have to demonstrate that the economy actually always gets much worse when a Republican is in office. But mainly this claim fails to take into consideration a vast amount of other factors that can affect the economy, such as policies enacted by previous presidents, Congress, the public, and the private sector.

This example can be reversed, as presidents generally like to take all the credit for when the economy is doing well. When job creation is up and unemployment is down, presidents like to claim that the policies they enacted must have been the cause without providing any real evidence. They essentially claim that because the economy is doing well and they are the president, they caused the economy to do well. This is bad reasoning and an extremely oversimplified explanation for the ups and downs of an economy. Remember that demonstrating a relationship between two events requires related facts to back up the claim.

Tuttle Twins Takeaway

This fallacy is more helpful to recognize when you are going about your daily life. Sure, it will be beneficial to understand this fallacious reasoning when facing an opponent during a debate, but you will find you recognize it around you all the time. Critically thinking about various events that happen in the world and providing a reasoned based understanding for *why* those events possibly occurred will keep you from falling into this trap.

APPEAL TO EMOTION

It's difficult to debate an opponent who uses emotional manipulation instead of valid arguments. Although emotions are powerful, they don't necessarily lead to logical or correct conclusions.

What About the Children?

During a debate, it may feel like you're losing the argument or the crowd is losing interest. It's important to present your arguments in an engaging manner, but this can be a difficult skill for some. But you must avoid falling to the temptation of adding some spice to your argument by committing a very common fallacy: the *appeal to emotion*.

It can be tempting not only for you to present emotion in place of reason but also to allow your emotions to be manipulated by appeals to emotion made by your opponent. Appeals to emotion try to make you or your opponent have feelings of empathy, fear, hatred, and more. This is a wrong-headed attempt to replace reasoning with emotion.

Here's an example you might have experienced as a kid. You are sitting at the dinner table with your family. Your dad has cooked up some yummy looking burgers with some disgusting looking Brussels sprouts on the side. You quickly eat up the delicious burger but maybe sit there with a disgusted face at the thought of eating Brussels sprouts. Eventually, you proclaim to your parents, "I'm full. I cannot eat those awful Brussels sprouts."

Maybe your parents sometimes say no problem, but surely at some point your parents fallaciously used some appeal to emotion, telling you to think about the poor, starving kids who have to beg for their next meal, who would be so happy to have a fulfilling warm meal. How do you think they feel?

Now you can recognize this for what it is: an appeal to emotion.

Obviously, you were not avoiding eating the Brussels sprouts because you wanted to disrespect children in need. The problem is that your parents used emotion to manipulate you. In reality, a fake argument wasn't even used; the use of an emotional story holds no actual logical reasoning. They used an appeal to your sense of pity to convince you to accept that you should eat Brussels sprouts. They evoked the use of emotions in place of evidence for the benefits of eating the Brussels sprouts.

The appeal to emotion is commonly used in more serious real world areas such as politics. If you are looking for an exercise for helping to recognize appeal to emotion, political speeches are filled with them. They oftentimes attempt to make you angry and fearful of your current situation or, more generally, the country's situation.

Politicians love to use emotion to paint a picture of why you should vote for them instead of the opposition. They use emotion to convince you to support them or donate to them. Why? Because an appeal to emotion often works, even though politicians typically fail to provide solid reason-based arguments. But another important reason for understanding the appeal to emotion is to help you build your skillfulness in presenting an argument.

Another important understanding in argumentation is that an appeal to emotion isn't always bad. Humans are emotional creatures; we are easily manipulated through emotion. The politicians recognize that these emotions keep us attentive. In argumentation, your number one priority should be presenting a solid, reason-based, logical argument. That said, the addition of a well-placed emotional story can help earn attention and sympathy from your audience.

An important distinction, however, is that the emotional appeal doesn't replace your argument. It's used as extra material after your well-reasoned argument has been presented. Remembering to focus first on establishing a solid and logical argument will keep you on the path of understanding ideas and principles presented to you. Learning to recognize the wrongful use of emotional appeal, then learning to properly use the tactic in a meaningful and helpful manner will set you on a path towards skillful argumentation and communication.

The appeal to emotion consists of the following three parts:

- Person A states their position.

- Person A expresses an emotional story intended to invoke an emotion.

- Person A concludes that, therefore, you should accept their position.

An Example with Ethan and Emily

"Ethan and Emily! Wait up!" Samuel yelled from across the park.

Ethan looked over curiously, "Hey, Samuel, what's up?"

Samuel was out of breath after jogging over to Ethan and Emily. "Not much. Just thought I'd check to see if you two were down to play with me and some friends?"

Emily noticed he was carrying a drink she hadn't seen before. "What's that drink you have?"

"Oh, it's this new soda that came out. It makes you happy, keeps you in shape, and doesn't have the bad health effects of other sodas," Samuel responded with delight.

Ethan and Emily exchanged skeptical looks.

Ethan responded, "Samuel, what makes you so sure this new soda is healthy for you?"

"Well, I saw a TV ad for it and this really muscular dude was drinking it with a group of friends and everyone had a smile on their face. And then the muscular dude said, 'This is not like any other soda!' So if a fit guy like that is drinking it, it must be good for you," Samuel said to Ethan with a smirk.

Ethan and Emily exchanged even more skeptical looks.

"I don't think it's a good idea to trust a TV advertisement. They just want you to buy their product," Emily explained.

"You guys just don't get it. The new company has to show how their new product makes you feel and look," Samuel responded with a surprised look. "Well, I'll just let you two miss out," he said, turning to jog away as he sipped his soda.

The twins exchanged one final look of skepticism. Mouths agape, the twins were left to wonder what had just happened…

What Happened?

You should always be skeptical of advertisements. Never take them at face value. Samuel took the ad literally. But the advertisement is an example of an appeal to emotion. Advertising uses it all the time to convince you to share or buy. Advertising is presenting an argument to garner an emotional response from you, the consumer.

Samuel allowed his emotions to get the best of him. He failed to recognize that he had fallen prey to a fallacious argument made by the soda company. The soda company had used imagery in their advertisement to invoke happiness from the consumer, not to convey facts.

And, unfortunately, the advertiser won the debate by using bad reasoning. They used emotional appeal to push Samuel into action by using a muscular dude and happy people to convince him that "this could be you." Samuel had become convinced that he should buy their product. But a reason-based argument wasn't made; a pure appeal to emotion had taken its place.

The second issue is Samuel then tried to convince Ethan and Emily to buy the drink by explaining the exact same appeal to emotion that the ad did. This is what a well-thought appeal to emotion does; it convinces you and moves you to act.

Imagine a family event taking place shortly after a tragic school shooting occurred in your state. During a political discussion with the family, you suggest that the answer to school shootings isn't more gun control, because it hasn't worked in the past. Instead, a better understanding of mental health would prevent people from acting out this way. Your uncle disagrees and interrupts you saying, "How dare you want innocent children to be slaughtered at the hands of these death machines!" He goes on that you should think of the children and claims you would feel differently if it was your friend or sibling that was killed in a school shooting.

Of course, you don't support innocent children being killed, and your uncle hasn't presented you any evidence for why a better understanding of mental health isn't the answer. Instead, your uncle wanted to argue for increased gun control by appealing directly to emotion using one of the most popular appeals: the children. Your uncle never provided logical reasoning for why gun control would help. You may have noticed an uncomfortable feeling just reading this example, so be sure to avoid its improper use on others.

Tuttle Twins Takeaway

First you must learn to understand the appeal to emotion is not meant as a tool for establishing good logic and reason. Learn to use good logic first, and reason in argumentation of ideas, then allow the use of emotion to become part of your progression. Once you understand this, you can then use emotion as a tool for better argumentative communication.

SLIPPERY SLOPE

Rather than addressing your argument head on, a person using this fallacy shifts the focus to an extreme hypothetical that likely won't occur, hoping that people's fear of the hypothetical scares them away from agreeing with you.

Businesses would self-regulate if they were held liable when their products do harm.

All production would stop from fear of litigation.

Price controls during catastrophes can lead to supply shortages.

But without price controls, prices would soar to unlimited heights.

Gambling shouldn't be a criminal offense!

Everyone would gamble if they didn't fear punishment.

Slide When Ready

You might have heard your parents warning you of the consequences of an action, but sometimes, the consequences they describe seem a bit extreme. For example, "If you don't get your grades up, you'll fail out of school and end up with no job and eventually be homeless!" Your parents care about you and want you to do well in school, but in this case, they relied on a slippery slope argument to try to make their point. Just as the name implies, the slippery slope fallacy suggests that a particular action will lead directly to drastic end results.

A slippery slope fallacy assumes that A will lead to B which will lead to C, and so on. Although B and C might be possible results of action A, the presumption that it will lead to B and C might not be true. The problem with this type of argument is that it isn't always based on facts, but on assumptions of what will happen. It also tends to exaggerate the aftermath of one decision or action.

Have you seen the film *A Christmas Story*? In this holiday classic, a young boy named Ralphie hopes to wake up to a "Red Ryder Carbine-Action Two-Hundred-Shot Range Model Air Rifle" on Christmas morning. When he finally gets to tell "Santa," he tells Ralphie, "You'll shoot your eye out, kid!"

This famous line is a prime example of a slippery slope, which relies on a major assumption that Ralphie will act irresponsibly with the air rifle and injure himself as a result. And using this fallacy, the store Santa jumps to an extremely detrimental circumstance to justify why Ralphie should not have the air rifle.

This is problematic because it is an attempt to use a worst case scenario as evidence but the over exaggeration undermines his argument.

It's a large leap in reasoning to go from Ralphie receiving the air rifle to concluding that Ralphie will eventually shoot his eye out. Even though it is hypothetically possible that Ralphie could actually shoot his eye out in particular circumstances, Santa has presented no *evidence* for why he believes Ralphie will inevitably shoot his eye out. So the best way to counter the use of the slippery slope fallacy is to learn to recognize its use and simply call attention to it by explaining that they actually haven't presented any evidence for their conclusion.

There are times a slippery slope could be necessary in an argument, but you must provide evidence that one result will lead to another.

Say you are in an argument with your mom about whether or not you should get a job over the summer. She wants you to work, but you don't.

You tell her, "If I get a job, then my grades could be negatively affected because I'll have less time to study for math, which I'm close to failing. Then, I will have to sit out of my soccer games, because I won't have a high enough grade point average to qualify for the teams. I really don't want to miss any soccer games."

Your use of a slippery slope could be justified, because— in this circumstance—it's not completely unreasonable to assume these things could happen, and you have made a reasonable attempt at providing evidence for why one claim could lead to another.

If you had instead said, "If I get a job, my grades will drop, then I will fail out of school, lose all my friends, and end up as a failure in life," the conclusions you rely on for reasoning are preposterous. Plus, you haven't provided any evidence.

It's important to recognize a proper use of the slippery slope argument is when evidence is presented for why a *slip* could occur. You must learn to recognize this because in its proper use, the claims and evidence must be refuted for good argumentation. Also, at times, you may want to properly use slippery slope reasoning in an argument. Presenting these slippery slope claims with proper reasoning becomes a must, especially because of the fine line between proper and fallacious use.

The slippery slope fallacy is commonly presented in this form:

- Person A presents "If A, then B. And if B, then C."

- The trend continues, and ultimately it ends with Z.

An Example with Ethan and Emily

Ethan and Emily had a long day at a theme park, riding roller coasters and swimming in the wave pool. They were exhausted when they got home, and Ethan announced, "I'm going straight to bed!"

"Aren't you forgetting something?" Emily teased. "Like your teeth?"

Ethan sighed and told her he'd brush his teeth tomorrow.

Looking puzzled, Emily said, "Well, if you don't brush them now, they'll turn black and fall out!"

Ethan shrugged his shoulders and walked back to his room, too tired to wonder what happened.

What Happened?

Emily relied on a slippery slope fallacy to support her claim that Ethan should probably brush his teeth before he goes to bed. When Ethan replied that he would wait to brush, Emily responded with drastic and ridiculous claims, and failed to provide supportive evidence or explanation of her reasoning. Although there is a chance that Ethan's teeth could turn black and fall out if he fails to brush them over time, the possibility of that occurring is extremely small (especially overnight!). Therefore, Emily probably shouldn't rely on these extreme outcomes as support for her claim.

Many people jump to provide extreme outcomes when explaining why a certain action should be taken or avoided. It's easy to do, but should be avoided because using this tactic makes your argument appear weak, with no real supportive reasoning for what you're trying to argue.

Consider the state of Colorado, whose voters worked on a ballot initiative to legalize recreational marijuana use. Preceding the vote, arguments between proponents and opponents were frequent. Although both sides likely committed slippery slope fallacies along the way, consider a fictional opponent, Marybeth, who might have said something along the lines of the following:

"Marijuana is a terrible drug and if recreational use was legalized, it would result in teenagers addicted to smoking the plant which would lead to the zombification of nearly all of Colorado youth who would become too lazy to attend school and instead stay home and experiment with more and more drugs, which will lead to high death rates and criminal activity in teenagers."

Marybeth's arguments probably come off as ridiculous, and that's because of the way she presented them using the slippery slope fallacy. She jumped from one extreme conclusion to the next, without stopping to provide reasoning for any of them. Although there is a chance that teens could become addicted to marijuana or criminal activity may rise, she provides no evidence as to why that would happen as a result of marijuana legalization. These claims are extreme, and if they are going to be made, an explanation needs to follow for why one thing leads to the next. Instead, by claiming one detrimental outcome after another, with no connection in between, she appears to be a non-credible source who relies on scare tactics rather than reasonable facts.

To avoid this fallacy, she could have taken a step back and made a series of progressive explanations, taking time to offer the evidence for why she thinks each one will occur. For example, perhaps she thinks that criminal activity will rise because drug users are frequently arrested in the U.S. In her mind, that must mean that most drug users are involved in other criminal activity, and by legalizing a drug, legalizing access would mean more users and thus create more criminals. Although this reasoning is false, it still functions as an explanation which provides her opponent and audience with some evidence about her assertions. Plus, once she explains all her claims and how they connect to one another, she may realize some of her assertions are wrong.

If you decide to use a slippery slope, it's important to be aware of how you use it and make sure you reasonably connect all your arguments. Make sure that the claims you are making are not so drastic that they appear irrational.

Tuttle Twins Takeaway

The most important takeaway of the slippery slope fallacy is recognizing the drastic and unrelated jumps in reasoning. When you are making well-reasoned arguments, you must always provide evidence of why one claim leads to another. That's just good debating! Learn to point out fallacious jumps in reasoning by making sure you provide proper reasoning for why one claim leads to another. You can successfully recognize this fallacy by learning to see and make reasonable *steps* in your argument. Always justify why one claim leads to another.

AD HOMINEM
Latin for "To The Person"

Whether it's an overt attack against a person, or a more subtle casting of doubt on their character, someone using this fallacy tries to undermine a person's argument without having to address it.

Leave My Character Out of This!

Imagine you are back in kindergarten, and you and your playmates are hanging out at the park. Some drops of water begin to fall from the sky, so you all run inside the park's pavilion to protect yourself.

Once inside, your friend David says, "It's sprinkling outside."

But then your other friend, Ally, looks over and says, "No, it's raining outside."

They go back and forth about the right word until David delivers the final blow by saying, "Ally, you're just an idiot!"

David has introduced the *ad hominem fallacy*. This fallacious tactic essentially boils down to an attack on someone's character or personal traits as an attempt to undermine an argument.

Imagine being in an exchange with another person, where you're presenting a logical and reasoned argument, only to have your opponent cut down your character, your looks, or something about you to the audience listening in on the argument. Not only is this offensive to you, but it adds nothing to the conversation of ideas at hand. Instead it raises unnecessary tensions between you and your opponent.

By claiming Ally is just an idiot, David is engaging in a perfect example of the fallacious ad hominem tactic. Instead of continuing the discussion, David has opted to only cause tension and has provided no reasoning to establish why his attack is relevant. This type of personal attack adds nothing to the dialogue, does nothing to address the argument, and doesn't add any reasoned-based evidence for determining if it's raining or sprinkling.

Of course, the example used is between children, and you will need to be equipped to recognize when teenagers or adults use this same fallacy more skillfully. Here's an example:

Tim thinks we should lower taxes, because it will help increase economic prosperity and innovation. But Allen thinks Tim shouldn't talk about politics, because he clearly doesn't know what he's talking about.

Now, looking at this example you see an adult-level discussion about politics. But when you compare this argument to the debate about rain between children, you can see the tactics used in the argument aren't so different. After someone presents a reason-based argument about why taxes should be lowered, Allen saying that Tim doesn't know anything about politics does nothing to address the original claim that was made.

Ad hominem arguments focus on information that is irrelevant to the discussion. The problem is that when you are in a debate with someone else and these personal attacks are thrown at you, the attacks can influence the audience. So it's vital to learn this fallacious attack and how to respond.

One of the best ways to counter this attack is to simply recognize the fallacy and point it out to your opponent. Tell your opponent the personal attack has nothing to do with your argument. Calling out your opponent can go a long way in influencing others. Go on the offensive and ask your opponent to make a justification for his personal attack. Why is it relevant to the discussion?

You should not stoop to your opponent's level. Do not counter their personal attack with a personal attack. This ruins productive dialogue and can reflect badly in the eyes of the audience. Plus, it only adds further tension between you and your opponent.

Acknowledge the attack and point out why it's not relevant to the discussion. It can go a long way in a conversation or a debate, earning you respect with observers.

The use of an Ad Hominem argument usually consists of the following three main parts:

- Person A states position X.

- Person B claims we can't follow Person A's position X, because Person A is dumb.

- Person B claims, therefore, that X is not true.

An Example with Ethan and Emily

"Hey, Marcos, I don't get why you never want to hang out with Amanda," Emily said as she leaned against a tree the group was hanging out at for some shade.

Ethan was curious about Marcos's reasoning as well, because every time Ethan and Emily wanted to hang out with Marcos, the twins wanted to be able to invite Amanda along as well. But Marcos always told them not to invite her because he wants to hang out with just them.

Marcos tried to explain, "I just can't stand her."

"You have to give us more than that," Ethan insisted.

"I don't know. Ever since she moved here, I've thought she was just arrogant and dumb," Marcos responded.

"I don't get how you think that. You've barely hung out with her," Emily quickly replied.

But the twins were left to consider what had happened.

What Happened?

Marcos failed to provide any reasoning. He decided to resort to child-like name calling. He put forward the idea that Ethan and Emily shouldn't hang out with Amanda, but his reasoning was based on the ad hominem attack of name calling. He then concluded that Ethan and Emily should accept his reasoning for why they shouldn't hang out with Amanda.

The problem is that Marcos hasn't provided a reason-based argument—merely an accusation about Amanda. This is one example of an ad hominem attack. But the ad hominem can come in various forms of personal attacks.

For example, imagine yourself in a conversation with your Uncle Joe, who loves to flex his political muscle at you. In the course of your conversation, you put forward the idea that you think we should decrease federal and state spending for public schools and reduce restrictions on private schooling options, because you think the current system of education is inefficient in finding cost effective ways to better educate the youth. Additionally, private options could be a better alternative.

What does your Uncle Joe have to say back?

You're just a crazy libertarian, so clearly we shouldn't listen to your ideas on education spending. Too extreme!

Instead of choosing to address your reasoning for a change up within the education system, your uncle chose to attack you personally. Even if you're not actually a libertarian, your uncle intended for the libertarian categorization to be a negative attack on you. Essentially, it's a more sophisticated version of child-like name calling.

Your uncle used unrelated information (libertarian) as information for discrediting your claim. You being a libertarian or not has absolutely nothing to do with the idea you brought forward, and it adds nothing to the conversation.

Let's take a step back and have a similar conversation with your Uncle Joe. You make the same reasoning for why you want to decrease federal and state spending for public schools and deregulate private schools. But this time your uncle has a slightly different fallacious tactic up his sleeve.

You're only saying that because your real motive is to abolish all government. You just want anarchy!

Do you see the difference? Instead of presenting negative information about you as a person, your Uncle Joe is dismissing your viewpoint because of what he perceives as your motives. This is still an ad hominem attack, as it's an attack on the *motives* of you as a person. The personal motives or characteristics of a person adds no reason-based information to disprove your original claim.

Maybe you've not experienced this, but at least imagine how it would feel. Not good. Remember that as you determine your course of action for presenting an argument. Personal attacks in general don't feel good, and it's not any different experiencing them after presenting a thought-out argument.

Tuttle Twins Takeaway

Consider the motivation behind the ad hominem attack. People don't like being personally attacked, which is what motivates people to use this attack in debate. Learning to remain calm after being on the receiving end of this fallacious attack will help in keeping the conversation on course. Keep the conversation focused on ideas by pointing out the logical flaw and irrelevance of the attack, then move back to arguing the ideas being discussed.

PERSONAL INCREDULITY

Just because something is difficult to understand, or you're not sure how it works, does not mean that it's not true.

"Think for yourself!" "Make me!"

No matter what arguments you make in life, there will always be someone who disagrees with you. Some will offer valid counterpoints, while others will simply plead ignorance, which is the fallacy of *personal incredulity*. This plea of ignorance or disbelief of your claim is used in an attempt to discredit your ideas.

Personal incredulity might occur when someone wants to avoid accepting new information. When presented with a well-reasoned argument, your opponent might just point out how something doesn't make sense to them. However, there's a difference between your opponent genuinely not understanding your argument and your opponent deciding they don't understand it or don't want to believe it simply because it doesn't support their claim.

You must learn to recognize this fallacy as your opponent will use it to discredit your claims. Imagine you overhear some friends arguing over whether God is real or not. The friend who denies God's existence asserts that if God truly existed, someone would have found a way to scientifically determine that He is real. Because the friend can't or chooses not to understand the other friend's faith, he flat out denies it.

Likewise, if you disagree with their reasoning and claim, then you must provide counter reasoning and a claim for why they are wrong. But if you simply say their concept or idea doesn't make any sense and you choose to not further inquire about their presented concept or idea, you're arguing fallaciously.

In a discussion, your opponent will likely ask for further details when they genuinely don't understand your arguments and claims. Remember that something being complicated does not necessarily make it untrue. When listening to claims, it's up to you and your opponent to educate yourselves about the claims being made or simply say, "I don't know." This is better for thoughtful discussion than just simply claiming something isn't true because you don't understand it. When entering a conversation around ideas, it's best to leave your ego at the door.

You have to keep in mind that your opponent might use the fallacy by accident. When this happens, continue to politely explain their fallacious reasoning with an expectation that they will be open to changing their mind. This way, you both can continue a thoughtful conversation around the discussion topic. This is not only good for the conversation between you and your opponent, but for the audience observing as well!

In time, you might encounter an opponent who continues to make ridiculous claims. When you've confirmed their claims are actually ridiculous, it's probably safe to think their next ridiculous claim might not be worth looking into. You are reasoning from your past experience with this particular opponent, using that as evidence for not believing a claim being made by them. You are not merely dismissing something you don't understand or don't want to hear.

When your opponent is a repeat offender of this fallacious reasoning, they're only wasting your time. They don't want to lose an argument, consider alternative viewpoints, or accept they might be wrong! Imagine your frustration when facing this type of opponent! Remember that before *you* claim your opponent doesn't make any sense because their claims don't fit your agenda.

In situations where your opponent isn't open to considering your explanation for why they were being fallacious, it might be best to just end the discussion or at least move to a new discussion topic. If your opponent isn't willing to change their mind and unwilling to consider alternative viewpoints regardless of the point you make, what's the point of continuing the conversation? Only continue the argument if you have a crowd of undecided and open minds willing to consider the concepts and ideas you present.

This fallacy is usually presented with two main parts:

- Person A can't imagine or believe X can be true.

- Person A claims something can only be true if they can explain or imagine it.

- Person A concludes that X must be false.

An Example with Ethan and Emily

Ethan and Emily were taking a language immersion class before their trip to Spain. It was coming down to their last few classes, so they had one big project left to go. After class they were talking with their friend Jeremiah, who also happened to be going to Spain, about the class.

"Ugh! This project is going to take me all weekend to complete. This Spain trip better be worth it," Ethan groaned.

"Yeah, luckily we can work on it together to figure it all out," Emily added in response to Ethan.

"This assignment doesn't make any sense to me. The teacher did a terrible job of explaining it, so I'm not even going to bother doing it," Jeremiah complained to Ethan and Emily.

"Well, you need to complete the assignment to pass the class and receive the certificate of completion," Ethan answered.

Jeremiah didn't seem phased or concerned by this. He responded, "Well, it's up to the teacher to explain the project better. The project just doesn't make sense."

The weekend went by and Ethan and Emily worked long and hard on their Spanish project for Monday. Jeremiah, on the other hand, came in to class on Monday empty handed because he did not work on the project over the weekend.

"Okay, it's time to turn in your final projects," the teacher announced to the class as she walked in the classroom door.

Everyone started handing their projects forward. The teacher looked over and noticed Jeremiah hadn't handed a project forward.

The teacher walked over to Jeremiah and put her hand on his desk, "So Jeremiah, where is your final project?"

Jeremiah looked up at the teacher and responded, "Well, I looked at your instructions for the project, and they just didn't make sense."

"Not understanding the instructions isn't justification for not doing the project," the teacher responded with a frustrated look. "For one, you could have asked me to clarify if you didn't understand something," she continued.

Jeremiah shrugged his shoulders and laid his head down. He did not pass the class. The twins were left to wonder what had just happened.

What Happened?

In this situation, Jeremiah made the teacher his opponent. He thought her explanation of the assignment was unclear. In a way, he sees her explanation for the assignment as an argument for whether he should or should not do the assignment.

Instead of doing the assignment, Jeremiah appealed to ignorance by claiming the assignment didn't make sense. He was likely making this excuse from a fallacious position, as he didn't *want* the instructions to make sense because he simply didn't want to do the assignment.

Jeremiah could have sought further explanation from the teacher, asked a classmate for more information, or simply made his best attempt at understanding the instructions. The problem was he wasn't open to a better understanding of the assignment due to laziness.

Someone's inability to explain or imagine how an idea or argument presented to them can be true doesn't make it false! This fallacious line of reasoning is commonly used in political discussions to dismiss claims that don't fit that particular individual's narrative. Imagine a conversation with your political Aunt Amy, who claims she doesn't understand how private schools can be good for kids. She says the only reason people and groups want private schools across the country is so that business people can profit off of them!

See the problem? Her inability to understand the benefits of private schools doesn't provide any substance to the argument. Not understanding how private schools can benefit kids doesn't change whether or not private schools are truly good or bad for kids. The use of the fallacy doesn't make the claim true, either, but is commonly used as a way for your opponent to support their own theory.

Tuttle Twins Takeaway

When you suspect your opponent is using personal incredulity, inquire further to determine whether they truly do not understand. If you determine that they are purposely arguing fallaciously, simply point out why their reasoning is fallacious and ask them to demonstrate the problem with your evidence. Remember it might be their lack of understanding, not so much the lack of information.

SPECIAL PLEADING

People don't like being wrong, so when it turns out they are, they'll often invent ways to cling to their old beliefs, including claiming that their position is an exception that is still true.

I'm really sorry that I dented your car hood.., ...**but** it was an accident and I don't have enough money to fix that.

A free labor market lowers prices for everyone... **Except** it isn't fair that immigrants, willing to work for less pay, should get my job.

I believe that we must restrain the government by being true to our inspired constitution... ... **but** this time we must trust the president.

Pretty, Pretty Please

When you're facing an opponent in a debate or argument, it might be tempting to make a quick response without considering the *best* response. Under the pressure of the crowd, you might have the urge to speak before taking a moment for thoughtful reasoning. This can result in arguments that make you appear uninformed on your issue or unreasonable toward your opponent.

The pressure to respond quickly can often lead to glorified begging. Imagine your friend takes you to his favorite psychic, Egnew Prophesie, who he claims is the best at predicting the future and revealing the past, "like magic." Although skeptical, you decide to give it a shot. When you get there, Egnew continually makes wrong guesses about your past and becomes disgruntled when her abilities are not seeming to work on you. In an attempt to explain her shortcomings, Egnew claims that you must not believe in her abilities, and that's why they've failed to work.

See the problem? Her claim is that she has psychic abilities, though when they failed to work on you, she made a special plea that it was because you don't *believe* in her abilities. In other cases, she always had success with her psychic abilities, because she was working with believers. However, when encountering a nonbeliever like yourself, she made an exception to her claim, saying that it must be because you don't have faith in her abilities. This is a classic case of someone using the *special pleading fallacy*.

The point isn't about whether or not Egnew has psychic abilities. It's about the fact that Egnew claimed that she had great psychic abilities. Yet, when presented with a situation that was counter to her narrative, she justified her claim by making a special exception to the rule.

Instead of considering possible reasons for her psychic powers failing in this situation, she began to scramble for a response. She fallaciously attempted to make a special plea to explain why her standard of accurately predicting her clients' past still holds true: it must be something wrong with you. Ridiculous!

Consider this more politically relevant example: A politician claims that anyone caught with cannabis or using cannabis should be thrown in prison. He claims that throwing cannabis users in prison will deter its use. The politician has set a standard by making the claim that people should be thrown in prison for using dangerous substances.

You might have already thought of a response to this claim: there is a substance that people are caught using all of the time—alcohol—which is a dangerous substance when used irresponsibly. Just look at the alcohol related driving deaths every year. The politician responds by claiming that alcohol is exempt because it's legal to use and doesn't lead to the use of other drugs, so people shouldn't be thrown in prison for using it.

The politician's argument is badly reasoned, in more than just one way, but the focus for this chapter will be the special pleading fallacy.

The politician presented an argument that the use of dangerous substances should result in prison time, with the intention that it be applied to cannabis. When presented with a counterargument that adults are already trusted to use alcohol, despite many instances of alcohol-related deaths and injuries, the politician responded with a special plea for why alcohol doesn't fit his standard.

Although the politician provided reasons, he still made a special exemption to his rule. The problem with his reasoning is that it wasn't relevant to the argument against the claim that alcohol is dangerous. Remember to address special pleas during a conversation by simply asking your opponent *why* their exemption from their set standard is justified. It's up to them, not you, to provide justification, but the same goes for you when making special pleas!

This fallacy contains three main parts:

- Person A accepts standards X and applies them to others in circumstance C.

- Person A also falls under X in circumstance C.

- But Person A claims to be exempt from X, so C is still true.

An Example with Ethan and Emily

Ethan and Emily were having their friend Marcus stay overnight at the house for the weekend. It was starting to get late.

"Hey, Marcus. Can you turn off the movie? It's really bright and loud, and I'm trying to get to sleep," Ethan kindly asked Marcus.

Emily added, "Yeah, could you please? It's getting very late."

"Why should I? It's not even that late," Marcus proclaimed as he continued to watch the movie and eat some popcorn.

"Emily and I just feel like going to bed," Ethan responded.

"Well, sorry, but I feel like staying up and watching the movie," Marcus said as he continued to watch the movie.

"I'm going to bed and you're going to turn off that movie. You must turn it off!" Ethan responded with some frustration.

Ethan and Emily went on to try and fall asleep while Marcus continued to watch the movie. Later they found an opportunity to consider what happened.

What Happened?

For starters, this an example of a more immature use of the fallacy. Both sides decided to make their own special pleas. Even though Ethan and Emily might be in the right in this situation as it is their house and they have the right to determine how and when their TV is used, this doesn't change the fact they used poor reasoning to make their claim.

Ethan and Emily wanted to go to bed, but Marcus did not. He wanted to stay up and watch the movie. The standard set in this situation was made by Ethan, who wanted to prove his point by simply insisting on his preference. In this case, Ethan *wants* to go to bed.

Marcus responded with the same standard that wanting to do something is reason enough for others to follow. So Marcus *wants* to stay up and watch the movie. Instead of Ethan deciding to use better reasoning, he falls back on fallaciously using a *special plea* that Marcus should just follow what he wants because he has some sort of special exemption from his own reasoning!

Ethan failed to resolve the conflict. He established a standard that he wasn't willing to follow and offered it up as a claim that Marcus should follow. Unfortunately, this is a common tactic in the world of public policy.

Imagine you are talking with your Uncle Mike about decriminalizing cannabis across the country. You put forward the claim that cannabis should be decriminalized because you don't think it's the government's place to stop individuals from doing something that isn't harming others, concluding that cannabis users shouldn't be thrown in prison.

Your uncle disagrees and claims that cannabis users are lazy and the plant is a gateway to more dangerous drugs. Instead of decriminalizing, he says, "We should throw users in prison as a deterrent!"

In this situation you seem to recall your uncle discussing how he used cannabis just a few years ago. You bring up this information and ask your uncle if he thinks he should have been thrown in prison if he was caught with cannabis.

Your uncle claims that of course he shouldn't have been thrown in prison, because he was responsible and never used more dangerous drugs. Your uncle has just committed the special pleading fallacy. Many people who use cannabis illegally probably don't think they should be the ones going to prison because they are "responsible" or don't deserve to go to prison. Nobody thinks they deserve to go to prison! Remember to consider the standards your claims lead you to accept. If you don't follow the standard yourself, why should others?

Tuttle Twins Takeaway

You always need to remember to back up your claims! You should learn to recognize this fallacy so that you can quickly call out your opponent when they don't want to accept their own standard. But also consider what the claims and standards you put forward to opponents forces you to accept. If you are unwilling to accept the consequences of your arguments, are those arguments or ideas thoroughly and properly considered?

LOADED QUESTION

Don't get set up by your opponent—these questions "load" a negative proposition within them, which attempts to make you look foolish or guilty no matter how you answer. It's a trap!

Do you know how fast **you were speeding?** You look nervous. **What are you hiding? How much** do you hate me right now ?

Only a **loser** would be a Tigers fan. You're **seriously** rooting for them? How can you like a team **that's so lame?**

Locked and Loaded

"Eat your vegetables or go to bed." "If you don't do your homework, you can't go to the football game this Friday." These types of ultimatums aren't uncommon for parents to give their children. At some point in your life, you were probably offered a similar choice from a parent or teacher. For some, these choices might feel like a trap, with neither option feeling favorable. Sometimes during an argument with an opponent, you might be presented with a similar type of entrapping question—the *loaded question*.

For example: *Have you stopped cheating on your tests?* The question is a loaded question because it assumes information about you: you've cheated on tests before. This type of question makes you appear guilty simply by just answering the question.

If you were to say yes, you've just admitted to cheating on tests before. But if you were to say no, you would not only be admitting to cheating on tests before but also admitting you still do!

Imagine this tactic being used in a debate, where you are presented with a loaded question by your opponent. This tactic might be used to trick you into providing a reaction-based response and make you appear bad to your audience.

This is a common tactic used in media interviews. They try to make the person unintentionally make a statement that will be negatively perceived to hurt the person's reputation. This is all in the pursuit of encouraging more people to read their headlines or click their links, for more advertising revenue and attention.

You must learn to recognize when a loaded question is being asked. The question forces you to agree to a claim that you disagree with or is a question that limits your pool of answers. Plus, it's often used to imply a negative perspective about you, getting you to accept negative personal attributes simply by the phrasing of a question.

One way to answer these loaded questions is to stop yourself from intuitively answering with a yes or a no.

When faced with a question like "Have you stopped cheating on all of your tests?" Instead of answering yes or no and trapping yourself into a corner, take the time to reply with extra clarifications, such as, "I have never cheated on any of my tests." By doing so you call out the fallacy by denying both of the implied answers.

Simply calling out the fallacious reasoning or question in this case can go a long way in earning trust from your audience. Plus, if your opponent is looking to have a reason-based discussion of ideas, they will be willing to accept when you've properly pointed out fallacious reasoning on their part. In the case of the test, simply say it's wrong of your opponent to assume you have cheated without any evidence! If you intend to further your discussion, do this with kindness to keep your opponent from shutting down to the ideas presented in your arguments.

The loaded question fallacy essentially comes down to one basic part:

- Person A asks a question to Person B that assumes information about Person B.

An Example with Ethan and Emily

Ethan and Emily were hanging out at the park with their friend Kendall when they noticed the new person in town, Kylie. She had just moved here a couple of weeks ago.

"Hey, look! It's Kylie," Ethan said as he saw her car pull up to her house across from the park, "We should see if she wants to hang out with us."

"Yeah, she seems cool. Let's ask her. But wait. Emily, do you still hate her?" Kendall turned to Emily as he looked at her with a stern face.

"What? I don't hate her. I only met her one time, and she seemed very nice," Emily explained.

"Huh. You just seemed to not like her when you were with me when we met her. You had an odd look on your face," Kendall remarked with his arms crossed and a slight shoulder shrug.

Emily looked at Kendall with a little frustration, replying, "Well, you can't just assume I hate her. What kind of question is that?"

"I'm just going off of what I saw, but whatever," Kendall said just before running over to Kylie to ask her to hang out.

The twins were left to wonder what just happened.

What Happened?

To start, notice the similarities between the loaded question presented by Kendall and the one from earlier about cheating on a test. The question is intended to get a quick reaction, to have the person fall into the trap of admitting something they never intended to admit. This type of questioning acts as a "trick question," where the question is solely used to garner a response.

The question doesn't actually have a correct answer. These trick questions or loaded questions can also be used merely to draw controversy to the situation. This was the case with the question Kendall asked Emily, as Kendall likely knew his question would illicit an angry response whether or not Emily actually answered him. It seemed to be intended to get "under her skin" and get her frustrated.

Let's bring it back to a more real-world example to help explain this fallacious tactic. Take this question:

Do you actually support this insane president?

This loaded question contains a claim within the question. In this case the question claims that the president is insane. The fallacious nature of the question occurs because by merely answering the question you cannot refute the claim within the question. So this question acts as a trick question to get you either to support an insane president or not support him, yet think he's an insane president.

Another common use of the loaded question is using a statement, then following with a question that's supposed to back you into a corner where you feel foolish to not accept their statement. Take this fallacious situation:

Intelligent people know not to believe what the media has to say. Do you believe the media?

In this case, the claim put forward prior to asking the loaded question is intended to back you into a corner. If you answer their question with a "yes," their statement claims that your answer makes you unintelligent.

One way to avoid using this tactic yourself is to look for times when you use a loaded question and then proceed to break down that question into smaller questions. This allows you to confirm information about your opponent to avoid upsetting them and steering the conversation off course. Look at the question about the sanity of the president. Instead, ask your opponent if they think the president is insane. Confirm that answer and follow up by asking if they support the president based on the information that was confirmed prior. This way you can ask questions to help move the conversation without making careless claims.

Tuttle Twins Takeaway

You must learn to avoid using this fallacy, because it can irritate your opponent due to its appearance of being trickery. Additionally, using this fallacy assumes you have knowledge about your opponent that they might have never agreed to. Wrongly assuming information about your opponent can not only upset them but upset the audience, as they might see you as a slimy debater. If you want to be able to have thoughtful and insightful conversations about a broad spectrum of ideas, you must learn to argue with respect for your opponent and those watching. Learning to recognize this fallacy will help you properly phrase a question without assuming information.

BURDEN OF PROOF

When a person runs out of evidence to support their argument, they may try to explain that a lack of proof only shows that their claim cannot be disproven.

The Proof Is in the Pudding

In a discussion, you might come across an opponent who thinks their idea is so innovative that it's your responsibility to disprove their claims. This might sometimes happen when your opponent becomes blinded by outside information that doesn't fit their narrative. Plus, their arrogance begins to get the best of them during a discussion of a broad range of ideas, and they begin to think they have the ideas mastered and it's up to you to prove them wrong!

Enter, the *burden of proof fallacy*. Imagine that your Uncle Mike tells you that on Europa, a moon of Jupiter with a surface completely covered in ice, there's a mermaid-like alien colony just below the surface. You might be wondering, what evidence does he have for this? As a good debater should, you interject and ask for the evidence. Your uncle responds by saying, "Well, you can't prove me wrong!"

Based on our current technology, you cannot truly prove beyond a reasonable doubt that mermaids don't live under the ice surface of Europa. But does this make your uncle's argument strong? Do you have good reason to believe his claim? No. Just because you can't prove something wrong doesn't mean it's right.

One way to understand the fallacious reasoning behind your uncle's claim is to understand what it is that this type of reasoning and logic forces you to accept. Take the mermaid example, except let's make it a little more crazy: instead of mermaids, it's a colony of swimming centaurs that shoot laser beams from their fingertips. This is a ridiculous claim that is very likely false, although it would be kind of cool if true. Yet, it's not technically falsifiable at this time, because of limitations in our technology.

We know that the surface of Europa has ice but we don't know for certain what's below the surface! You should not take every claim seriously that you can't prove false. Remember, when someone makes a claim, the obligation is on your opponent to support that claim. You don't immediately have an obligation to prove them false if they've failed to provide reason-based evidence to support their argument. If your opponent claims that the burden of proof is on you to prove them wrong after they make a claim, they are likely committing the burden of proof fallacy.

This fallacy often occurs when a bold claim is made, such as mermaids living inside Europa. One way to prevent yourself from falling to the temptations of this fallacy is to avoid the thinking that everything must have an answer now, when in reality we are constrained by our limitations of knowledge. Stay open to new ideas, to a reasonable extent, especially ones that have some practicality.

Luckily, people often have a common-sense understanding of this fallacious tactic. When someone makes a claim, people look for that person to provide evidence, especially during a discussion of various knowledge-based topics!

For example, you don't have people going around claiming that pigs can fly and then just end the conversation. When someone makes an outrageous claim like that, they will likely understand that they will have to provide proof to back up the claim. Whether the reasons for the claim are good or bad is less important for understanding this fallacy; the point to remember is that the burden of proof is on your opponent after making a claim, not you.

This fallacy is usually presented in two types of ways:

- Person A claims X.

- Claim X has not been disproven.

- Person A concludes that X must be true.

Type two is usually presented with four basic parts:

- Person A makes claim X.

- Person A asserts that X is true if X can't be disproven.

- Limit of knowledge prevents the disproving of X.

- Person A concludes X is true.

An Example with Ethan and Emily

It was around Christmas time; Ethan and Emily were at their annual family gathering for the holiday. As usual, they hung around their cousin Timothy, and some holiday motivated conversation ensued.

"Do you guys believe in Santa Claus?" Timothy asked Ethan and Emily while eating Christmas dinner.

"Nope, our parents told us all about it a few years ago, though I was suspicious before," Ethan explained.

"Yeah, I figured it out when Ethan did," Emily added.

"Well, I still believe that Santa is real," Timothy proclaimed as he continued to eat.

Emily looked over at Timothy with a confused look and asked, "Didn't your parents tell you?"

Timothy responded, "They just told me Santa isn't real and left it at that—no proof. I bet you can't prove me wrong either, so my claim is right!"

Ethan lifted his head up from his soup and responded, "Do you honestly think a bearded man delivers presents to every house in a flying red sleigh every Christmas, and he lives at the North Pole, which is a bitterly cold place?"

Timothy responded with a stern look, "First of all, Ethan, you've never been to the North Pole, so you can't be sure that Santa doesn't live there. Second, are you seeing every single house all over the world to see who is giving everyone presents?" He then added, "So since you can't possibly know if he doesn't exist, then what I said is right!

Ethan and Emily became frustrated with this, and the three of them finished their meals in an awkward silence. Fortunately, Ethan and Emily had a chance afterwards to consider what happened.

What Happened?

Timothy used the burden of proof fallacy by shifting the burden onto Ethan and Emily. In some cases of its use—like the example with mermaids on Europa—the person making the claim is saying that because nobody can disprove their claim, the claim then holds true. In the case with Timothy, he shifted the burden of proof and claimed his opponents (Ethan and Emily) were not able to prove that Santa Claus doesn't exist.

Another issue with the fallacious burden of proof tactic is that once your opponent begins going down this path, it will lead to more and more claims that involve the same faulty reasoning. Imagine that the conversation with Timothy continued with Ethan and Emily using satellite imaging as reasonable proof that there is no evidence of anyone living at the North Pole.

Timothy might have countered that Santa used his magical powers to move his toy factory below ground to avoid satellites. Then, Emily might respond by pointing out that Santa would technically have to stay hidden forever and be unable to deliver his toys! If Ethan were to push on these claims, their cousin would likely say that they can't prove his claim is wrong with absolute certainty. In a way, he's not wrong because of the limits of our knowledge; however, this doesn't make his claims true.

Essentially, Timothy's claim ends up being a string of continually fallacious reasoning that only wastes the twins' time and his time. Honestly, if you're really good at making long intricate strings of imaginative claims, you should consider writing fiction.

Tuttle Twins Takeaway

As always, you want to keep your conversations on track! Learning to recognize this fallacy is a must because using it can lead down a path of continuous shifting of their argument and reasons why you must be the one to prove your opponent wrong. This constant shifting of the goal post is a waste of your time and your opponent's. Remember, take a step back and consider who made the claim and who has to prove it.

AMBIGUITY

Language has its limitations. Some people will purposefully mislead others, or say something that can be interpreted in more than one way, so that they can later point out that they were not technically incorrect when challenged.

Starstruck

A clear and concise explanation of your claims is the best way to present an argument. However, as made apparent in many chapters throughout this book, it is evident that individuals often stray from good argumentation tactics. They may do so by using confusing language to trick you into accepting their conclusion. This strategy, whether used intentionally or not, is called the *ambiguity fallacy*.

The ambiguity fallacy comes in various forms, and you will have to familiarize yourself with its assorted uses. Consider the following: When you look into the sky on a clear night, you see an abundant amount of stars. What you are looking at, scientifically speaking, is thousands of exploding balls of gas. Justin Bieber is widely recognized as a star. Therefore, Justin Bieber is an exploding ball of gas.

Obviously this example is ridiculous, but it explains what this type of faulty reasoning can back you into accepting. Each line of reasoning was technically true: Justin Bieber is probably the most recognizable name of our generation, which would make him a star. And stars are exploding balls of gas. The problem is each time the word star is used, it holds a different connotation. If you were to break down each individual line of reasoning and replace the word star with its appropriate definition, the statements would appear disconnected and result in a failed argument.

Consider a more realistic use of the ambiguity fallacy: a news organization claims it has a duty to print stories that are in the public interest. The news organization then claims the public has an interest in politicians and political commentators. Because it is an interest of the public, the journalists come to the conclusion that reporting on rumors and stories that haven't been confirmed is still within the news organizations duties.

See the problem? In this example the news organization is ambiguously using the word *interest* by using it with two separate meanings. The first uses interest in a way where the news organization has an obligation to the public to report on news that benefits the public as a whole. The second use of interest refers to the public enjoying reading or hearing about juicy stories and rumors about politicians and political commentators.

If your opponent were to use this example, they would be committing the ambiguity fallacy because they have shifted the meaning of a word or phrase to fit the conclusion they want you to accept. In the news organization example, it probably doesn't benefit society to spread baseless information about politicians and political commentators. This argument might be used by a news organization to justify their questionable actions, but it's up to you to point out the fallacious reasoning.

Sometimes this fallacy occurs because of bad grammar, but bad grammar does not mean you commit the fallacy of ambiguity! Sometimes bad sentence structure and wording that is included accidentally with reasons and claims of an argument. For example: last night I saw a flying pig in the sky with my pajamas on.

Is the speaker saying the flying pig in the sky was wearing the speaker's pajamas or that the speaker was wearing pajamas while watching a pig flying in the sky? Your opponent is less likely to use this type of ambiguity on purpose but more likely by accident. However, being able to recognize this fallacy during a conversation will help clarify your opponent's point and help them learn to be better at explaining, which will help the progression of the conversation as a whole!

Psychics commonly use confused wording and grammar on purpose when making predictions. The more vague a psychic makes their predictions, the more likely the prediction will be perceived as coming true, which empowers them in their business. Fallaciously empowering them, that is!

Remember during your conversations to clarify your positions when necessary, whether that be your own positions or asking your opponent to do so. This will help the progression of conversation and avoid the accidental use of the ambiguity fallacy.

The fallacy is usually presented with two parts:

- Person A uses reasoning and premises with unclear language that allows for more than one conclusion.

- Person B draws a conclusion from that reasoning.

An Example with Ethan and Emily

Ethan and Emily were hanging out with their friend Samuel and his girlfriend Nikki at the local high school's track meet. It was a hot and humid day in May, and you could see the heat was affecting the runners.

"I cannot imagine having to run long distance on a day like today," Ethan said to the group.

The mile race was about half over, and the runners were

starting to look drained from the scorching heat.

"Wow, the runner who just ran by looks super hot!" Nikki proclaimed.

Samuel quickly turned his head over to Nikki, "Excuse me?"

Ethan and Emily looked at each other, sensing a tense situation between Samuel and Nikki starting to develop.

Nikki looked at Samuel and explained, "What do you mean? The runner looked SUPER hot!"

Samuel started to get red in the face. "I can't even believe you."

He got up and walked away, believing that Nikki was physically attracted to the runner.

Nikki, looking confused, said to herself, "What? The runner looked like he was about to fall over from heat exhaustion."

She got up and dashed after Samuel, leaving the twins to wonder what just happened.

What Happened?

Samuel clearly misinterpreted what Nikki meant when she said the runner was "super hot." He wrongfully assumed that Nikki was complimenting the runner's looks, which made him upset and jealous, when she was actually just commenting on the runner's temperature. It was an error of communication that could happen to anyone if they jump to conclusions rather than clarifying what was actually meant.

The ambiguity fallacy is used in the world of politics quite often. Imagine that a family in your neighborhood called your state senator to complain about cars speeding in the neighborhood. The senator is sympathetic towards their arguments and runs a bill to heighten the penalty for speeding. When presenting the bill on the senate floor, the senator claims, "This is a very concerning issue my constituents have asked me to fix. I represent the people of my district and want to make change so they feel safer."

What the senator said was technically true, constituents did in fact bring him this issue. But he uses constituents in a way that wrongfully suggests that many people in his district reached out about speeding. In reality, the number of constituents was actually just two, a concerned couple with small children.

The senator tactfully decided to use the broad term of "constituents" rather than "two people in my district" because the latter is less powerful and convincing. This argumentation tactic can be called out if another person simply clarifies by asking the actual number of constituents who reached out.

Tuttle Twins Takeaway

Throughout your conversations about ideas, you will need to explain your thoughts concisely and clearly. Part of this is recognizing and avoiding the ambiguity fallacy, as this can be helpful to not only you, but your opponent. Having the ability to pinpoint a location of confusion in your discussion will help continue the progression of the debate. Also, remember this fallacy can occur in your opponent's line of reasoning without ill intent. A confusing situation could simply be boiled down to confusing sentence structure!

The GAMBLER

There are actual calculations that can determine the odds of something being possible, but when the laws of physics, nature, and logic are replaced with imaginary reasoning, what you're left with is just a game of chance.

The Fallacious City

Have you been to Las Vegas? The entire city was built on people continually having fallacious internal arguments with themselves. This fallacy is most commonly linked with gambling, hence the name the *gambler's fallacy*. It's a basic fallacy that you must come to understand to avoid some very negative consequences associated with it!

Imagine playing a coin toss with your friend Rebekah. You must guess what the next coin toss outcome will be, either heads or tails. You toss a coin and it lands heads up five times in a row.

Rebekah asks, "What do you think your next toss will be?"

You tell her tails, because you've flipped five heads in a row, and the chances of that is so unlikely that a tails will probably be next. To you, the outcome of landing on tails is long overdue. However, you have just fallen prey to the gambler's fallacy.

You determined your next prediction as though the coin has a memory of past events. You thought that previous outcomes of the coin flip will predict the future outcomes, even though you know that there are two potential outcomes and the coin is neutral to previous events. You thought the previous coin tosses somehow affected the outcome of the next event. This is fallacious reasoning, as the next coin toss is independent from what happened before. No matter how many times you flip the coin, the next coin flip remains a fifty-fifty chance for either heads or tails.

The gambler's fallacy can function in the opposite direction as well. In the case of the coin flip where you had five heads flipped in a row, some may think that the coin is "on a roll" or "on a hot streak" and that the next flip is likely to be heads. Again, this line of reasoning sees previous flips as a prediction for future events, but a coin flip has an independent outcome every time; it will always be a fifty-fifty chance.

Comparing this coin flipping game to gambling, you can see how this fallacy is commonly committed. Gamblers create an illusion of control, where they think that they can predict the next outcome. It's important to learn to recognize this fallacy to avoid allowing it to cloud your judgment and keep your ability to reason in top shape. The gambler's fallacy has an emotional appeal, because people want to comfort themselves by creating an illusion of control. In reality, it only blinds them and helps casino owners make lots of money.

In a city like Las Vegas with gambling based purely on probability all around you, this fallacious mistake can be costly, both mentally and financially. You must recognize situations where the odds are random chance. Avoid the false illusion of control or the thought that you have the ability to predict outcomes when this ability is nonexistent.

The gambler's fallacy usually comes in three basic parts:

- Random event X happened.

- Person A predicts random event must self-correct.

- Person A concludes random event X is more/less likely to happen.

An Example with Ethan and Emily

Ethan and Emily were facing one of the most frightening yet important moments in high school — taking the state driver's license test. Before the test, their classmates gathered outside the classroom to quickly cram as much last-minute knowledge as they can. Every second counts, right? As Ethan and Emily exchange thoughts about the questions, their friend Marcela chimed in.

"I'm done cramming," Marcela said confidently. "Now I'm just getting firm on my strategy for when I have no idea what the right answer is to a multiple-choice question! If I'm clueless, I'll just pick a letter I haven't chose in a while. You're more likely to get it right that way!"

Ethan curiously responded, "So if I have a string of A's, say four in a row, should I go back and change my answers?"

"Absolutely! The chances of having four A's in a row are unlikely," Marcela replied with a stern look. "I always use the results of my past answers to help determine my next one. It's commonsense probability."

Emily was confused, responding, "Yeah, but shouldn't you base your answers on the actual answers the letters represent?"

"Yeah, but we all know the letter distribution is going to be roughly the same," Marcela replied. "Well, do what you want, but I'm going to use my tried-and-true predictability skills. Good luck!"

Marcela failed the test.

Later, Emily and Ethan had an opportunity to discuss what had happened.

What Happened?

In this case, Marcela looked at the driver's test as being some sort of predictable game where she could determine the next outcome based on previous answers. Her argument has some other flaws as well, because not only is her probability indicator off, her understanding of test taking is as well. For one, the answers on the test are determined by whatever the exact answer is.

Marcela essentially assumed the test would have an even split between the letter answers and thought that was more important than the actual answers to the test. Additionally, she got the probability issue wrong. The test was absolutely random, so the previous question's answer choice had nothing to do with the current question's answer choice. Marcela saw each question as dependent upon the past. However, you know that each question's letter value is independent in each question.

So Marcela was committing the gambler's fallacy because she failed to see each question of the test as independent. Instead, she viewed each individual event as a chain of connected events. In this case, she created an illusion for herself about test taking, which has made her less effective at reasoning properly, which would help her become a better test taker.

Now imagine a slightly different case of your aunt and uncle arguing over lottery tickets. They both love playing the lottery, but in this case one was very upset with the other. Your uncle chose the numbers 1, 2, 3, 4, 5, but your aunt picked 48, 56, 89, 123, 345. Your aunt was furious because she claimed your uncle chose a number string that is much less likely to occur than hers.

Your aunt reasoned that if the number "1" was picked first in the lottery, the number "2" would not follow. She sees a number outside of the chain being much more likely, but she has fallaciously tried to claim she could predict, based on previous outcomes, the next outcome of random choice. In the lottery, each time a number is picked, they are chosen from a pool of all of the numbers, which makes every single number have equal probability of being chosen during every decision.

Tuttle Twins Takeaway

The most important takeaway for the gambler's fallacy is simply learning to recognize it. This fallacy is most common in your internal reasoning, not necessarily as much of an aspect with arguing or debating an opponent. So you must remember to recognize areas of life or games that rely on independent cases to determine probability. And you must avoid the emotional appeal to make an illusion of control when one doesn't exist.

The
BANDWAGON

When new ideas challenge your current way of thinking, reasoning through them can be difficult and sometimes uncomfortable. It's a common reaction to pass this responsibility onto others.

If Everyone Jumped Off a Bridge, Would You?

Sometimes you may face an argument that seemingly everyone believes. Arguments that seem to have a consensus should not be off limits in terms of debate. Issues that have dominant public support for one side over the other can have people wanting to "jump on the bandwagon."

The *bandwagon fallacy* is when someone tries to use the popularity of a particular side of a debated issue as a reason to support an argument. In the middle of a debate, you might reasonably think that because one side is so popularly approved, it must be right. This appeal to popularity can be tempting in the heat of the moment, but you must remember to address their argument.

The problem of using this appeal to popularity is that it's done nothing to address an argument, strengthen an argument, or undermine an argument. So by using this fallacious tactic, you've wasted time and have not come closer to the truth of the idea at play.

Take an issue that holds almost unanimously popular support: *We know the earth isn't flat*. The fact this opinion is popular has no bearing on whether or not the earth is round or flat. Instead, we know the earth isn't flat because we have pictures from space from different angles, and you cannot fall off the edge of the earth. Those are just a couple of the many reasons why we know the earth isn't flat.

Presenting the scientific reasoning for the issue is the logical route to take. The popularity of that scientific reasoning doesn't add anything to the argument.

People often inflate the popularity of an issue as evidence. But let's go back to our popular conclusion that the earth isn't flat. Now, if we were to put ourselves into a time machine and travel back hundreds of years ago and ask people is the earth flat or round, what would the answer be? The popular answer among people would be *the earth is flat*.

So if you were to use or accept the fallacious bandwagon fallacy as good reasoning, the popularity of the belief that the earth is flat during that time period would mean the earth was actually flat. Not only is this fallacy weak reasoning, but it's not a reason for a conclusion at all, which makes its use a waste of time because instead of proving your point, you show the audience a weak understanding of the issue. It does nothing to prove your conclusion, only that the conclusion is popular.

The use of the bandwagon fallacy usually consists of the following three parts:

- Person A states their position X.

- Person B holds position Y because it's popular.

- Person B concludes position Y is right because it's popular.

An Example with Ethan and Emily

Ethan and Emily were hanging out with a large group of teens in the neighborhood. The twins were only really good friends with Carlos but thought it would be fun to get to know and play with some other kids in the neighborhood.

Ethan, Emily, and Carlos walked up to the other group of nine neighborhood teens.

Carlos introduced Ethan and Emily, "Hey, guys. This is Ethan and Emily. They live in the neighborhood."

Nate introduced himself to Ethan and Emily, "Hey! Nice to meet you two. We're about to go play some soccer in the park if you want to join."

Ethan and Emily both responded, "That sounds fun! Let's go."

Adam, another guy in the group, skipped the introduction. He said, "Hold up, hold up. We always play five on five with soccer."

"We could play six on six," Emily suggested.

Adam looked to Emily, crossing his arms, "Well, it's more fun playing five on five."

Nate responded to Adam, "I think it would be more fair and nice if we played six on six today."

Carlos nodded in agreement.

Adam looked at the rest of the group. "Do you guys want to play five on five?" he asked while his arms stayed crossed.

All of the group nodded in agreement with Adam.

Nate looked at his other nodding friends, a little confused. "Well, looks like everyone wants to play five on five. Sorry, Ethan and Emily," he said shrugging.

Carlos looked at Emily and Ethan. "Sorry you two, but everyone wants five on five. I'll see you later," he said, running over to his bike and waving back at the twins.

The neighborhood group rode their bikes away from Ethan and Emily towards the park, leaving Ethan and Emily wondering what happened.

What Happened?

To start, it seems that Ethan and Emily might not actually want to hang out with Adam and his friends, given how quick they were to exclude the twins. But let's look at the actions taken by Nate and the twins' friend Carlos.

In this situation, Adam had the popular support—more people agreed with his position for playing soccer five on five. As for Nate and Carlos, they started on the side of Ethan and Emily for putting forward that the group should play six on six soccer so everyone is included. Once Nate and Carlos realized the majority support was in favor of playing five on five they "jumped on the bandwagon."

Instead of Nate and Carlos sticking with their original argument that it would be better for everyone to play six on six, they accepted defeat. The problem is that Nate and Carlos could have presented further reasoning for playing six on six, such as it's the right thing to do to include everyone. Instead, they gave up on their argument and fell to the majority.

Maybe this situation makes you think of the old saying, "If everyone jumped off a bridge, would you?" Considering this scenario might be helpful if you are ever in a situation like Nate and Carlos.

This next example provides an important opportunity to help clarify the bandwagon fallacy—the case of a popular vote. In a democracy that has a popular vote for president, you might reasonably perceive the vote as a form of bandwagon fallacy.

With democratic elections, specific candidates or politicians are presented to the voters to choose as president and the person who receives the most votes wins. Therefore, the specific politician with the popular support should be president. What's wrong with this idea?

You must remember that logical fallacies are faulty arguments. In an argument, you have premises and a conclusion formed from those premises. When talking about the results of an election, the important distinction is that an election isn't making an argument; a system cannot make an argument. You can make an argument for why a particular system is bad, but the system itself cannot be fallacious, therefore it cannot commit the bandwagon fallacy.

However, the individual voters within a democracy can commit the bandwagon fallacy in relation to how they cast their votes in the election of a politician. If a candidate comes across as popular, and a friend then tells you to vote for the popular candidate because they are popular, your friend is engaging in a bandwagon fallacy.

Another example of a bad case for a popular vote in democracy would be if we were to jump back in our time machine and go back a couple hundred years and hold a democratic vote to determine if slavery should be legal or illegal. What do you think the outcome would be? A couple hundred years ago, most voters would have supported slavery here in the United States. Does this make slavery morally justified? No, the vote provides zero reasoning for the conclusion.

The point is that the fact that something is popular holds no moral basis or logical basis for the conclusion of an argument.

Tuttle Twins Takeaway

Fight this fallacy by ignoring whether or not an idea is popular. Falling to an appeal to popularity is the lazy way out of an argument. Additionally, falling to this fallacy only shows your audience you have a weak understanding of your preferred position. The best way to learn and progress is to consider ideas both popular and unpopular. In doing so you force yourself to understand the reasons and positions of both, which will help you win a debate of ideas.

APPEAL TO
AUTHORITY

Certainly the opinion of wise, knowledgeable, and successful people can be used to support a position—but not as a replacement for logical arguments.

Respect My Authority!

It can be difficult to organize your thoughts on the fly. Good arguments require research and thought, and during a conversation or argument, you have to be able to organize those thoughts quickly. This might tempt you to fall back on using the arguments of so-called experts on a topic as evidence for your case, instead of the research itself. Enter the *appeal to authority fallacy*.

Think of the authority figures around you: parents, teachers, coaches, or relatives. When you use the opinions of these authority figures rather than actual facts to support your case, you are engaging in the appeal to authority fallacy.

Imagine yourself in a conversation with a friend. During this conversation, you start debating whether dogs are better than cats. In this case you decide dogs are better, while your friend claims that cats are better because they are more laid back and lower maintenance. You counter his position by claiming that your dad says dogs are better, adding that he is very wise about the benefits of certain pets.

The problem is, your appeal to authority that your dad says dogs are better adds nothing to your original conclusion. Instead of offering an argument, you've offered the claims of an authority figure as proof that your belief must be true. Your dad holding the authority label does nothing to prove or disprove the evidence brought forward by your friend that cats are better.

This fallacious argument wastes time. If anything, you've lost credibility to your friend and anyone listening when they notice you haven't brought forward any ideas or arguments. For example, in the case of dogs being better than cats, a much better claim to make to support your point would have been that dogs are typically more playful than cats. Even if your friend disagreed, at least something was brought forward that could be addressed by your friend.

Imagine a similar situation with much higher stakes and real world implications: your friend Jason thinks abortion is morally acceptable. You decide you disagree completely but ask Jason why he holds his position. He responds by saying Dr. Roberts holds the belief that abortion is always morally acceptable. So, because Jason sees Dr. Roberts as an expert, he agrees with him.

In this argument, the stakes are much higher, as you're dealing with a highly divisive and political issue. You respond to Jason by acknowledging you've never heard of Dr. Roberts, and ask who he is. Jason says he is a doctor of industrial engineering.

Jason has appealed to authority by name-dropping a doctor as reasoning for why you should hold his position and why he does. However, Dr. Roberts doesn't address any moral reasons to be pro-abortion. On top of this, Dr. Roberts is an expert in industrial engineering, not medicine, and his expertise doesn't translate into his being an expert of morality or ethics.

Jason was looking to name-drop an expert to push his political opinion onto you. Unfortunately, political debates are a common arena for logical fallacies. The goal always becomes to achieve victory, rather than the discovery of good ideas. This win-at-all-cost mentality leads to the use of authority figures as support for reasoning. If your goal is to learn ideas, discover truth, and become a great debater, then you must learn to identify and avoid using an appeal to authority.

The use of an appeal to authority has three main parts:

- Person A says Person B claims X about a subject.

- Person A claims Person B is an authority on the subject.

- Therefore, X is true.

An Example with Ethan and Emily

Ethan and Emily were hanging out with Deven at the pool. A police car drove up to the pool parking lot, and the driver waved over at Ethan, Emily, and Deven.

Deven quickly sprang up and ran over to the cop car to greet the driver. They talked for a couple of minutes. As Deven jogged back through the pool gate, the police car drove off.

Deven sat back down next to the twins.

"Who was that?" Ethan asked with some curiosity.

"Oh, that's my dad. He's a police officer," Deven responded.

"Oh, wow! I had no idea your dad was a police officer," Emily said. She then glanced over at Deven with a curious look on her face, "So what advice has your dad given you, since he's a police officer and all?"

"Great question. That's easy: always, I mean always, do exactly what the police officers say. That's what he always tells me to do if a police officer asks me to do something."

"Hmm...I don't know about always," Ethan said curiously with his hand on his chin. "My parents told me about our right to refuse a search if pulled over and a warrant hasn't been issued. I think in that case it would be best to refuse. What do you think?"

Deven responded, "Well, my dad is a police officer and he knows the law. If he said I should always do exactly what police officers say, I'm going to do it."

Deven continued with frustration, "You shouldn't question a police officer, especially one like my dad, because if he said it, it must be true."

Later in the day, Ethan and Emily brought up what Deven had said about his dad and wondered what happened.

What Happened?

Deven and the twins provide a dialogue here that allows us to point out some key distinctions about the appeal to authority. Deven presented a claim made by his dad, who Deven assumes is an authority on the issue, on what should be done if a police officer orders you to do something. He claimed you should always follow the orders of the police officer, because that's what his dad told him.

Why is this an appeal to authority? Deven essentially made a statement—"you should always follow the orders of a police officer"—but then his reasoning for following this statement was an appeal to authority and bad reasoning.

Just because Deven fell prey to this fallacy doesn't mean the claim is necessarily wrong; his claim could be true. The fact his dad is a police officer—an authority figure—does nothing to prove or disprove Ethan's claim that we should always follow the instructions of a police officer.

You might be thinking, didn't Ethan use an appeal to authority by name-dropping his parents? In a way yes; however, the important difference in his argument is his appeal to authority was not used as a reason for accepting his conclusion that you should not always do exactly what police officers say. He brought up that your legal rights and the need for a warrant are important reasons to refuse the orders of a police officer.

Fallaciously using the appeal to authority occurs in argumentation, but you may reasonably rely on authority all of the time. We rely on authority figures for basic facts and information every day. For example, lawyers, doctors, parents, and professors—to just name a few—provide us information that you can reasonably trust as true without committing a fallacy.

Ethan's use of authority was an example of a proper use in argumentation. In his case, he is young and not an expert on the issue of police officer conduct. As for his parents, they are adults who likely have enough understanding of their basic constitutional rights for him to rely on their reasoning to refuse a search from a police officer. He was presenting an argument provided by an authority figure, not using the authority figure as his argument.

But Deven wasn't actually making an argument, and that's the problem. He was relying purely on the perceived authority (expertise) of his dad being a police officer. He presented his reasoning that way from the start, and when Ethan provided a rebuttal to his claim, he doubled down on his reasoning—his dad's expertise trumps Ethan's reasoning.

Tuttle Twins Takeaway

Fight this fallacy by focusing on facts and reasons for a conclusion, not the authority figures presenting those facts and reasons. Learning to separate the authority or expert on an issue from their respective arguments will help in learning, judging, and understanding the ideas being presented. This doesn't mean to put aside who made the arguments but to focus directly on the claims of that argument. By doing so you will better understand the ideas and learn to recognize when others commit the fallacy of appealing to authority.

COMPOSITION & DIVISION

We often observe consistencies, and sometimes might incorrectly *presume* consistency by thinking that when something is true for the part, it also must apply to the whole.

Native Americans suffer from the highest rates of poverty in the country, therefore all indigenous people need benefits for their economic disadvantages.

Media coverage of the investigation was full of biased misinformation.

So all media coverage must be lies, including this tornado warning!

Are Chickens Invisible?

During a debate you might face an argument that appears to be well-structured with reasoning that seems to flow well to its conclusion. In these cases you will have to quickly contemplate the content of the argument to avoid falling for faulty reasoning. For this chapter, the *composition* and *division fallacies* have been grouped together because their fallacious reasoning is so closely related. We'll start with the composition fallacy then move to the division fallacy and connect the two in the end.

Let's take a look at the fallacy of composition first. Consider this assertion: *Arizona is a state with a desert, so that means every state must have a desert!* The problem is that this assertion assumes Arizona being a state means *every* state must have the same qualities as Arizona—in this case, the quality of having a desert.

The assertion took a quality obtained by part of the whole—Arizona—and then applied it to *every* state. You might realize this is obviously not true given a basic understanding of the United States' landscape and climate. But look at an even more ridiculous example to help: you can't see cells without the aid of a quality microscope. Chickens have cells. So that must mean you need a microscope to see chickens.

No! Insanity!

This is what it means to assume that an attribute of a part of something must be applied to other parts of that whole. You don't want to be forced by your opponent to accept that chickens are invisible to the human eye!

On the fallacy of division side, the same misuse of reasoning occurs, but the defect in reasoning is that parts of the whole have the same properties as the whole they make up. Take a look at your friend's car, for example. Their car is black and old. Now, consider the individual parts of the car, like the engine. Does the engine being a part of the car mean that the engine must be black and old? Obviously not, because you can install a brand new engine that is silver in an old car. But that is what this type of reasoning forces you to accept!

A similar example is how individual car parts are relatively lightweight compared to a whole car. The attribute of all the individual car parts being lightweight doesn't transfer to the entire car, as you know that cars are really heavy. Applying this attribute of the individual car parts to the whole car is a fallacy from composition.

Another way to apply it is in reverse: the whole car is heavy for a human, so that must mean each individual part is heavy, too. Of course, you know this to not be true. A spark plug is part of a car, but it can easily be carried in the palm of your hand. It's obviously not as heavy as a car.

Learning to quickly recognize this fallacy is important during a conversation with your opponents. If you are conversing with a thoughtful and intelligent debater, they could pinpoint the faulty reasoning. Plus, if they were to demonstrate your bad reasoning to a crowd, they might point out that this type of thinking makes you believe in invisible chickens! This would be a little embarrassing, so avoid its use and its use on others.

The composition fallacy is usually presented with two main parts:

- The parts of whole A have qualities X, Y, and Z.

- Therefore, all parts of whole A *must* have qualities X, Y, and Z.

The division fallacy is usually presented with three main parts:

- Whole A has the properties X, Y and Z.

- D is a part of A.

- Therefore, D also has the properties X, Y and Z.

An Example with Ethan and Emily

Ethan and Emily went to their local minor league team's baseball game on a beautiful Saturday evening with their friend Peyton. This, of course, led to some discussion of baseball.

"Ah, I love watching and going to baseball games," Ethan said. "I think it's the best part of summer."

"Yeah, I agree it's great," Peyton replied, "I love watching the Yankees. They have all the best players in the league, so they will for sure be the best team!"

"Are you sure having the best players will make them the best team?" Emily curiously asked.

"Yeah, having the best players will make them a lock for the best record in the league," Peyton proclaimed back to Emily.

"I don't know. I think another team might just have players

that play better together as a whole," Ethan suggested.

The conversation continued, but Ethan and Emily had an opportunity to later consider what happened.

What Happened?

Peyton made her claim based on the fallacy of composition. She asserted that because the players (parts) on the Yankees are the best in the league, that the team (whole) would be the best in the league. She didn't address Emily's correct objection to her claim—that having the best players doesn't necessarily mean you will have the best team. The individual players all being the best players doesn't mean when they come together they will be the best team.

Consider this example from the fallacy of division, where your opponent makes the claim that the American court system is a fair and balanced system. Your opponent then concludes that because of this, criminals will always receive a fair and balanced trial. In this case your opponent distributed the attributes of the whole to each part that makes up the court system—the people who go through our court system. A reasonable position that could be argued for is that our court system generally is a fair and balanced system, but this doesn't mean every case within that system is therefore fair and balanced, as you can have a few bad cases while maintaining a generally fair and balanced system.

For good measure consider one more argument that is commonly used in political debates about immigration. Your conservative friend tells you to take a look at our country: it's made up of a bunch of houses, and people control who may come in and out of their own house. Their next assertion is that the country is like a house for everyone! Therefore, we should control who comes in and out of the country like the people do with their homes in the country.

With both the composition and division fallacy the *structure* of the arguments being presented is not the problem. It's the direction the attributes are assigned that is problematic. Take this famously used example:

All men are mortal.
Socrates is a man.
Therefore Socrates is mortal.

In this example the argument properly follows from each other because the attributes are correctly distributed. In this case, all men are actually mortal. So if Socrates is a man, he must be mortal. In order to be a member of this specific group (men), you must hold the specific attribute of that group, being mortal.

Remember that the content of the argument is what matters. When you examine the content of the argument you can better determine if those characteristics are able to be transferred to the other parts. This will have to be done on a case-by-case basis, but learning the structure of the fallacious argument will help in analyzing the content being presented.

Tuttle Twins Takeaway

When in a conversation or argument with your opponent, you will need to quickly consider the reasoning behind their claim. So practicing recognizing this fallacy in everyday conversation will help in those think-on-your-feet moments. Practice analyzing the content of the reasoning presented for a conclusion. Remember, it's okay to ask your opponent to clarify a connection in particular attributes of the parts and whole of various groups and objects.

NO TRUE SCOTSMAN

Instead of addressing a criticism of or flaw in their argument, sometimes people will dismiss it through an appeal to purity.

"Art is a multibillion dollar industry.

It doesn't need state funding."

But real art is usually funded by the state.

"Socialism has turned that once thriving country into a humanitarian catastrophe."

That isn't true socialism.

"Republicans are responsible for most of the nation's deficit spending."

Then they are not true Republicans.

The Goal Post Scramble

When playing a game of soccer, you have a reasonable expectation that the rules of the game will be followed, especially the most basic rules, such as maintaining two teams with a goalkeeper on both sides of the field. In this soccer game, imagine if someone stood by the goal post throughout the game, and every time you went to kick the ball, that person would move the goal post so you couldn't score. Frustrating, right? They're violating the basic rules of the game.

What does this have to do with fallacious arguing? Well, the moving of a goal post every time you set up to kick at the goal is a *no true Scotsman fallacy* of soccer. The no true Scotsman fallacy is a fallacious argument tool used to avoid criticism. In the case of the soccer game, whenever you attempt to score a goal, the opposing team *redefines* the location of the goal so you never stand a chance of scoring. This makes it impossible for your team to win the game.

Let's flip this analogy around and apply it to a discussion of ideas. The goal post is the claim or claims that your opponent sets up. After listening to your opponent's claims, you should address the claims being made. That's good arguing and leads to thoughtful discourse. Moving the goalpost would be like your debate opponent redefining their position after you've begun to address their points.

By moving the goalpost, or changing their claim, your opponent is essentially saying your claims don't truly address their original argument.

Here's a more real world example to help explain the fallacy: Douglas declares that all Scotsmen wear kilts. His friend Boyd points out that he's a Scotsman and doesn't always wear a kilt. Frustrated with his friend, Douglas responds that all *true* Scotsmen wear kilts.

You see? Douglas has merely moved his definition of Scotsman to fit his subjective understanding of what it is to be a *true* Scotsman. He adds subjective material to his argument on the spot to keep his argument free from attack, whether it justifiably addresses his claims or not. Merely redefining what it is to be a Scotsman when a counterargument doesn't fit your claim is a fallacious tactic.

When you think about it, it's a very arrogant fallacy to commit. By committing the fallacy you are essentially claiming you hold the ultimate authority on who and what is included in the understanding of a particular group. Committing this fallacy is also done to make you or your argument always look good.

One main issue with the no true Scotsman fallacy is that when discussing the positions of a group, anyone can define what a *true* Scotsman is or who *truly* fits the criteria to be a member of the group. You can probably generally define what it is to be a Scotsman but the threshold for a *true* Scotsman is much less clear. Sure, you may need some basic criteria to fit within a group of Scottish people, such as being from Scotland. But it's faulty arguing to displace members of a particular group simply because they don't meet someone's subjective understanding of who is or isn't a Scotsman.

This fallacious tactic can be convincing to a crowd of

watchers or readers. Learning to pinpoint and address its use is vital! Simply point out to your opponent that continually redefining their original claim does nothing for the progression of thoughtful discussion of ideas. Altering their claims to avoid counterexamples is like dismissing counterexamples simply because they are counterexamples.

This fallacy is usually presented with three main parts:

- Person A claims all X are Y.

- Person B provides an example of X not being Y.

- Person A refutes Person B by claiming that all true X are Y.

An Example with Ethan and Emily

Ethan and Emily were hanging out at their friend Christian's house. The TV was on in the background, with Sunday football on.

"I'm the Green Bay Packers biggest fan," Christian proclaimed. "I watch every single game… and every football fan must have a favorite team!"

"I think the Packers are my favorite football team," Emily said to Christian. "I really like their color scheme."

"I just like watching all the teams. I don't really have a favorite team," Ethan said as he shrugged his shoulders.

"Wait, wait, wait! First of all, Emily… Name one Packers player," Christian demanded as he tapped his foot.

"Well, I don't know, but I'm still a fan because I enjoy watching them!" she proclaimed as she glanced over at the TV.

"You are not a *true* fan if you can't even name one player on the team," Christian replied with a stern look.

"And if you don't have a favorite team, then you are not a *true* football fan," Christian said to Ethan as he turned towards him.

Christian quickly tried to change the subject, to put an end to the debate, as he continued to watch the Green Bay Packers game.

Ethan and Emily were left to consider what happened.

What Happened?

In this situation, Christian decided to fall back on the no true Scotsman fallacy twice; he argued that Emily is not a true Packers fan and Ethan is not a true football fan. His reasoning? They didn't meet his subjective criteria for what it is to be a fan of those particular categories.

His claim in general is about what he thinks it is to be an actual fan of football and an actual fan of a team. Looking at Christian's claim against Ethan, he sees having a favorite team as necessary to classify as a football fan—or *true* football fan.

But if Ethan were to come back and say that he simply enjoys the game of football and enjoys watching every team play, Christian would just reassert his original position by claiming that Ethan is not a *true* fan. He moves the definition of a fan to fit his viewpoint of who is considered a fan or not in order to make his viewpoint always the correct one. This makes objections to his claim impossible! This is not only lazy arguing but makes thoughtful discussion unachievable.

Instead of addressing Ethan or Emily's claim, Christian claimed he holds the ultimate authority on who is a Packers fan and who is a football fan.

Now imagine you are at a family reunion where Grandpa starts ranting about politics. He talks about how much he hates the two party system, and only 'fake' libertarians still believe in voting under this system. You respond to your grandpa by pointing out the need to vote on a state and national level to help push for the libertarian principles he holds. Your grandpa decides to respond by saying "true libertarians don't vote."

This is another example of the no true Scotsman fallacy. In this case you explained why you can be a libertarian while still deciding to vote. However, your grandpa chose to object to your claim by saying your point is not relevant to his claim simply because his example is talking about *true* libertarians. But this doesn't provide any substance for addressing your claim!

Tuttle Twins Takeaway

The no true Scotsman fallacy might be one of the best examples of a lazy argument. You might find your opponent using this claim when they are unable to address your counter points to their claims, which is probably a good sign you are saying something right! Avoid this fallacy, because it's an easy way to lose your opponent and crowd. The best way to address this fallacy is by simply pointing it out. Tell your opponent that they don't hold the ultimate authority of who or what is included within a group, which makes your criticism of their claims valid!

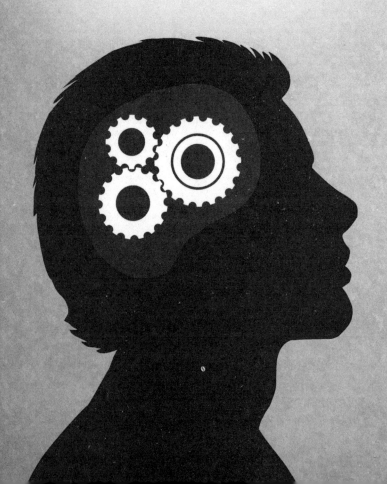

ORIGINS

Especially in today's world, it is difficult to know which sources of information are credible. That's why it's important to judge claims by their truthfulness, regardless of where they come from.

Corruption! Bribery! Oh, My! Fake News.

When you're in a conversation or debate, you have to think very quickly. This brings the temptation to slip into fallacious arguing. Don't do it!

In this chapter, we will discuss the lazy tactic of attacking an opponent's sources. This is called the *origins fallacy*. In this situation, you stumble to present a solid counterargument, so you attempt to discredit your opponent by attacking his source material.

When presented with well-researched ideas, it might become tempting to avoid your opponent's argument entirely, especially if you're struggling to think of a counterargument. Instead of attacking the argument, you might be tempted to attack the sources of the argument—where or whom it came from. By doing so you have fallaciously counter-argued their point by avoiding their main point entirely. This is slimy debating. It doesn't resolve the conflict or address the claim that was made by your opponent.

Consider the following example: A politician has been accused of corruption and bribery by a news source that has laid out a reason-based argument that he is corrupt due to a money trail they've discovered. When asked about these accusations, the politician exclaimed that the source was "fake news" and everyone should be cautious in believing the claims because "we all know to not trust the dishonest media."

See the problem? Instead of addressing the allegations presented by the media, the politician chose to attack the source of the argument, the media. His response made it about the origins of the argument, not the actual claims of the argument itself. Simply pointing fingers at whoever uncovered the story is not an argument to support the corrupt politician's claim of the media being untrustworthy. Remember what matters—the content *within* the argument, not the intent and history.

Avoiding your opponent's actual argument is an attempt to discredit your opponent with unjustifiable methods. And if your opponent happens to be up to date on their logical fallacies, you could be called out for your fallacious tactic. This causes you to lose trust with your opponent and the audience that listens or reads the conversation. Trust and respect are vital in an argument of ideas. Once you've lost trust, it becomes difficult for your opponent or the crowd to respect your ideas, no matter how good they may be.

Let's take a look at another case. Say a politician goes on a news commentary show to discuss a law that will lower taxes. The politician supports the bill because it will deregulate small businesses and decrease taxes for them, which he believes will help the state's economy. Someone else on the panel quickly responds by claiming, "You are only saying that because you've been bought out by rich and powerful corporations who want to keep money in their pockets."

This response shows the origin fallacy in use once again to attack the source of the arguments rather than addressing the arguments themselves. The activist assumed the politician was being paid to support the tax cut. Thus, he rejected the politician's claim simply because of whom it was coming from. Instead, the activist should have addressed the claims by making reason-based arguments against it, such as why he thinks the bill is bad for the economy. This fallacious tactic can come from the media and politicians alike, who put it to use at their convenience.

You need to address the substance of the argument. Learning to recognize the basic structure of the origins fallacy will help you avoid dubious tactics displayed by the politician and activist in the examples above. In the case of this fallacy, you must focus on the argument itself—the reasons and claims which are presented. The intent and history of the idea or opponent is a separate issue entirely, unrelated to the argument at hand.

The fallacy is usually presented with these three basic parts:

- Person A says X is true.

- Person B says Person A is a bad source.

- Therefore, X isn't true.

An Example with Ethan and Emily

Ethan and Emily were hanging out with their friends Samuel and Adam on the basketball courts.

"That was really fun playing pickup basketball, you guys," Ethan said to the group. "We should play again sometime soon."

The four of them had just finished playing a few games of basketball and were practicing some shooting to cool down afterwards.

"Hey, I was watching this YouTube video the other day, and it talked about how Earth is flat," Adam said as he dribbled the ball around. "Some of the arguments were pretty convincing. I mean my parents always talk about how dishonest the government is, and I agree, and I can see the government being in on the lie," he continued, shrugging his shoulders at the idea.

"Adam, those videos have been disproven time and time again. Plus we have photos from space showing that Earth is round," Emily said as she took a shot towards the hoop.

"No, no, no! Don't believe the lie! Those photos are obviously photoshopped," Adam hollered across the court, waving his hand at Emily.

Ethan and Samuel continued to practice their shots, but Samuel was becoming frustrated with the conversation he was overhearing.

"Emily, you can't believe a word Adam says. Everyone in the neighborhood knows his brother is a liar," Samuel said to Emily as Ethan quickly stole the ball away from him. "He is constantly making up conspiracy theories," Samuel continued.

"Come on, guys! Let's just play some basketball," Ethan insisted.

Later on, Emily and Ethan had an opportunity to consider this dialogue further and wonder what happened.

What Happened?

Adam presented a claim about why he believes the world is flat. Even though his information was not accurate, Adam did present an argument with his evidence about why he believes Earth could be flat. Emily countered with a reasonable objection to Adam's claim, pointing to the fact that we have hundreds of images depicting Earth as a sphere from the sky.

Adam quickly rejected this claim by mentioning the YouTube video had already discredited these photos as manipulated. Although Adam's source isn't credible, Emily handled the argument well by applying an objection to his argument and not the source. However, this was not the case with Samuel's objection.

Instead of countering Adam's claims, Samuel tried to discredit the *origin* of the argument. In this case he was using the simple fact that Adam is brothers with a source known to provide false information. However, you can think of Samuel's claim as independent from addressing Adam's actual points of Earth being flat. Even though you know Adam's claim is not true, using a fallacious argument to address his points doesn't create meaningful dialogue. Samuel's argument provides no reasoning to disprove Adam's points, only that Samuel thinks that Adam's arguments are bad simply because of its origin.

If we were to reimagine this scenario with Adam's brother as the one making the claims of Earth being flat, you could point out that you're skeptical because he has a proven record of providing bad or false information. That use of the origins fallacy would have more weight because you have *reasoning* for why the origins of the argument hurts the legitimacy of the claim. However, you should be careful at applying the origins argument unless you are sure you are using it properly.

Tuttle Twins Takeaway

Remember to always use a line of reasoning that relates to the *claims* and *reasoning* being presented by your opponent. When pinpointing this fallacy, recognize that the source of the material being presented is a separate issue from the claims being made by you or your opponent! The best way to keep a discussion on topic after this fallacy is used by your opponent is to merely point out that your opponent must provide reasoning for *why* the material's source matters. Make it your opponent's responsibility to demonstrate further reasoning when needed.

BLACK OR WHITE

It's often more comfortable for a person to believe that only two choices exist, and they might frame an argument that wrongly presumes this to be the case.

Excuse me. I'm taking a survey for the upcoming election.

Do you support Republicans or Democrats?

So...
...you AREN'T madly in **love** with me?

WHY, OH WHY DO YOU **HATE** ME SO MUCH?

What!? You don't support a universal basic income?

Well, then you want poor people to starve!

You are sick!

What's Wrong with Gray?

Imagine yourself witnessing an argument between two friends, both holding strong positions on their respective viewpoints. When the debate is going well, with thoughtful discussion between both sides, everything is good. But what if the argument becomes a little less peaceful?

With tempers raised, the once thoughtful argument tends to quickly turn into a fallacious yelling match with one goal in mind: winning the argument. This is especially common when one friend is a Republican and the other a Democrat. They both think their party is better than the other. Because they can't agree, they turn to you to decide the winner.

Imagine your friends putting you in this situation—that you have to choose if the Republican or Democrat party has the answer because they are the only two possible options. The problem is, your friends have just committed the *black or white logical fallacy*. They've presented you with two sides as the only possible choices, when in reality more options exist.

The Republican Party and Democrat Party have dominated our political arena for years, but they're not the only political parties that exist. You could choose the Green Party or Libertarian Party or even say you like to consider various political viewpoints and positions from all sides. When in a discussion of ideas, especially political ideas, you want all ideas considered.

This is a common fallacy in discussions, as people like to look at ideas through a lens of absolutes. You must learn to pinpoint this fallacy and address it. In order to do so, you must also recognize that in some cases two options might be all that is given for a reason. Consider an argument you might have once had with your parents when you were a kid: you want to stay up and play video games, but your parents present you the options to either go to bed or read for thirty minutes before bed. Maybe after learning about the black or white fallacy you would have countered by exposing their fallacious argument. But is this an example of the black or white fallacy? No.

In this circumstance, your parents are in an argument with you about staying up or going to bed. The key difference is your parents are well aware of alternative options, and they are not purposely misleading you into thinking other options don't exist. They are merely presenting you with two choices they would be happy with. In the case of your friends trying to force you to decide between Republican and Democrat views, they were purposely trying to mislead you into thinking those were the only two options in order to trick you into accepting their conclusion that one of those viewpoints is the answer. As your parents would admit, you can conceive of other options, such as staying up to play video games instead of going to bed. But they were giving you a choice to make, not presenting a fallacious either-or argument to trick you into accepting a conclusion.

Remember to have all possible ideas on the table! In the pursuit of knowledge and good arguments for that knowledge, limiting the information being discussed to only a few options can be harmful for your understanding of that idea.

The use of a black or white fallacy usually consists of these main parts:

- Person A has to choose either X or Z, even though other options may exist.

- Person A is not choosing X.

- Therefore, Person A has to choose Z.

An Example with Ethan and Emily

Ethan and Emily have just arrived at their friend Nate's house to hang out for some summer fun. Unfortunately, the weather did not want to cooperate on this summer day. The skies darkened as some storms had come in, keeping the twins and Nate stuck inside.

"Would you guys like to play some video games instead?" Nate asked eagerly. "I just got this fun, new open-world survival game. You two will love it!"

Ethan and Emily both replied, "Sure! Why not?"

The twins and Nate went down into the basement. Nate and Ethan played together first, as Nate only had two controllers.

After playing for about a half hour or so Ethan asked Emily, "Hey Emily, would you like a turn?"

Emily was getting bored just waiting around watching, so she quickly replied, "Yeah! Let me give it a try."

Nate brought the game back to its main menu so he and Emily could change characters. Emily started searching through the characters and noticed none of the characters were female. This never really bothered Emily before, but she wished she could sometimes play as a female character, instead of always playing as a male.

"Sometimes I wish video games had more female lead characters," Emily said.

"Well, as a male, I like males playing as male players and if they make more female lead characters then that means I won't have as many male lead characters to choose from. So I don't want any more female characters," Nate responded to Emily with an argumentative tone.

Ethan intervened saying, "But are those the only solutions?"

Nate responded, "Well, if the character is female instead of male, it's taking away the option to be a male character, that means fewer male characters for me to choose from."

The twins exchanged looks of confusion. The discussion had them feeling that something was missing and they wondered what happened.

What Happened?

Nate committed fallacious reasoning by viewing male and female characters as the only possible options. This misinterpretation leads him to another flaw in his reasoning, thinking that more of one extreme means fewer of another. In this case, Nate thought that more female characters in video games means fewer male characters. When in reality, game designers could simply add to the number of possible characters they create. His mindset was stuck between the two extremes he set up in his argument, as though those extremes were the only possible choices.

The other information his reasoning failed to take into consideration is the fact that main characters in video games don't necessarily have to be male or female. They could be aliens, robots, or something beyond your imagination. Point being, the black and white fallacy defeats Nate's own claim because he failed to take other information or ideas into consideration.

The failure to take other things into consideration is a common consequence of this fallacious reasoning. This fallacy can occur intentionally or unintentionally. Sometimes you commit this fallacy by purposely omitting viewpoints to convince your opponent to accept your conclusion. Other times you might think that only two particular options occur, when in reality more do.

Politics also happens to provide some perfect examples of this fallacy. For example, Republicans and Democrats love to position themselves as part of a group or team. This entices politicians to use language and rhetoric to invoke this feeling of "team support." Creating this mindset in political speeches, politicians proclaim you must be either for the party platform or against it, when in reality you can agree with some of their positions and disagree with others.

Imagine that your Uncle Joe presents the idea that in the system of capitalism, there is always a winner and a loser. He presents this as reason for avoiding an adoption of free-market principles. But you decide to respond to your uncle's statement by pointing outhow black and white his statement was.

Your uncle assumed that under capitalism, business always

includes a winner and a loser. In reality, when people exchange goods in a free market economy, you can have two winners. For example, when you go to the grocery store and buy fruit, the store receives money when you buy their product and you receive an item in return. Nobody lost. So your Uncle Joe failed to present a vital option in his argument's reasoning.

Like Nate in the dialogue with Ethan and Emily, your uncle failed to recognize alternative options within his reasons for his claim.

Tuttle Twins Takeaway

Remember, as always, the goal behind arguments and conversations is to gain knowledge. In this pursuit, you will want all of the information on the table. The only way to achieve this goal is not backing yourself or your opponent in a corner by accepting a conclusion based on the discussion of limited information. Taking a step back to gather well-thought-out research and information will lead you in the right direction for avoiding the black and white fallacy.

BEGGING THE QUESTION

Avoid using circular reasoning where you use the argument itself to justify why the argument must be true.

I Beg Your Pardon?

When you're arguing in circles, it's hard for the conversation to move forward. You just keep arguing the same point, or asking the same question, and nothing comes of it except frustration and maybe even resentment. But how does that even happen?

Take a moment and think about some of the questions you used to ask grown-ups when you were little:

"Why is the sun hot?"

"Why do I have to share my toys?"

"Why do I have to look both ways before crossing the street?"

Sometimes, the answer would be simple and you'd be met with patience by the grown-up. And maybe the simple answer would even be enough for you.

But other times, you'd be met with impatience or even be completely ignored. If the grown-up answered at all, they may have said something along the lines of "because that's how it is."

Sometimes, adults haven't thought through the answers to some of these "why" questions themselves, so the best answer they can give is "that's how it is."

That's not an answer, yet it's the kind of response we've all gotten at some point. We refer to responses like this as *begging the question* because the idea is also the conclusion. It's not even a weak answer—it's not an answer at all.

What would this look like in a debate? Imagine you're talking with someone about a set of ideas. Ideally, you'd be stating facts, arguments, thesis statements, and conclusions to get your point across, all in the hopes of convincing the other party of how valid your ideas are.

If, instead, you were to justify your argument with an argument—*you should share your toys because you should share your toys*—you would not be using sound reasoning. The argument used to justify the idea is assuming the truth of that very idea. Rather, it should be providing a sound explanation as to why the idea is true in the first place. Think about how the conversation would continue if the adult had instead offered a proper answer to the question.

Here's how this looks:

- Person A argues that X is true.

- Person B asks Person A why X is true.

- Person A states that X is true because of X.

An Example with Ethan and Emily

Emily, Ethan, Josie, and some friends were resting in the grass after having played cops and robbers in the twins' front yard. Emily was watching the cars pass on the street and began to wonder out loud.

"Why do we always drive on the right side of the road?"

Ethan looked over, his curiosity piqued. Josie piped up.

"There are lots of rules and the law says that we have to

drive on that side of the road."

"Yeah, but why?" Ethan asked. Josie frowned, unsure of what he was asking.

"My mom says because that's how it is."

The twins exchanged a confused look and turned back to their friend.

"Why?" Emily asked. Josie's frown turned into a scowl.

"Because." She stood up, annoyed. The twins didn't understand why she seemed to be getting angry.

"But why?" Ethan persisted. Josie huffed, really mad now. She stomped her foot.

"Because we *have* to drive on the right side of the road! Why are you asking me this?" Josie was so frustrated that she marched away, heading to her house. Suddenly, she twirled around. "The law is the law! Don't you know?" And with that final note, she flounced through her door, slamming it shut.

The twins exchanged a look, confused. What had just happened?

What Happened?

Emily's curiosity highlighted a very common, but careless, thought process in Josie: because Josie had no good answer, she justified facts, habits, and laws by accepting that "they just are the way they are" without trying to find a better response. When we do this, we're defending a so-called fact with that same fact. Just like "you have to share because you have to share," a statement like "you have to drive on the right side of the road because the law says so" turns into a never-ending conversation because the statement is also the conclusion. It goes in circles, which is why begging the question is also known as a *circular argument.*

Josie had no good answer herself, but she wasn't aware of it until the twins pushed for a better one, unwittingly emphasizing the fact that her statement was also her conclusion.

Generally, we don't realize that our argument is begging the question. After all, how often do we take the time to really think through the reasons why things happen ourselves?

Likewise, Josie had a conclusion and an idea that were one and the same, while Ethan and Emily had started thinking about the reason behind the idea.

Josie wasn't answering the question at all, but she also wasn't aware of it. Most of us don't realize when we're not actually making a point with our conclusion, either. It is an easy reasoning trap to fall into; most people use "that's the way it is" to avoid questioning the state of things. Maybe they don't care about it as much as you do, or they don't know the answer and don't want to admit it. Maybe they are just busy thinking about something else. However, your argument is moot when it believes the premise of the idea to be true from the start. It also means that you need to question your thought process from the beginning.

Instances of begging the question are hard to pinpoint in conversation, or even in our own reasoning, because we're assuming the truth behind the idea from the get-go. Realizing that the premise of our argument is none other than the argument itself is a challenge; questioning the truth of your own thoughts is even more of a challenging endeavor. It's hard to know what you don't know, isn't it? That is at the heart of the circularity of begging the question.

Tuttle Twins Takeaway

Be aware that even if something feels fundamentally true to you, your reasoning may not actually validate that thought. Fight this fallacy by asking yourself "why?" and seeing how far you can go with the answer. Just be careful: not everyone is welcome to having their ideas shown to be fallacious in their circularity, so choose your begging-the-question battles carefully.

APPEAL TO NATURE

Just because something comes from nature does not mean that it is good, justified, or correct.

The Nature of the Good

When you're in the middle of an argument, you need to constantly be on your toes so you can make thoughtful comebacks and rebuttals. In the thick of an argument, it can be tempting to fall back into using logical fallacies. One fallacy in particular seems to plague the minds of debaters discussing ethical discussions of right and wrong: the appeal to nature.

An *appeal to nature* occurs when you argue that because something is "natural," it must be good or valid. Essentially, you rely on nature as a reason for someone to accept your conclusion. This same reasoning is commonly used in the opposite sense: something that is "unnatural" is bad in some way. What makes using this fallacy so tempting?

Part of the reason is because there is a human obsession with the natural and unnatural. If you've seen any advertising, you've likely witnessed this fallacious argument tactic in use. The catchy phrases of "all natural" or "organic" are perfect examples of attempts at invoking this human bias towards accepting these phrases: the product is "healthy" because it's "natural." The problem is that just because something is organic or all natural doesn't make it healthy for you. The statement that something is natural or unnatural cannot validly prove, disprove, or support any conclusion.

Now consider this real world circumstance where something natural is actually quite harmful for you. You want to stay healthy. Marketers love to use natural and organic as code words to mean the food they are selling is healthy. But consider jasmine berries. They occur naturally on

Earth, but if a human eats these berries they can have nervous, respiratory and digestive system issues. They sometimes even cause death. The jasmine berries are natural but obviously bad for your health. It's easy to detect the faulty reasoning inherent in an appeal to nature when you're talking about poison berries.

Aside from being a misleading label for what is healthy, our understanding of the meaning of "natural" has changed over time. Same-sex marriage was once considered unnatural. Throughout history, most societies viewed it as unnatural. But today, society has largely shifted to believe that same-sex marriage should be accepted; it's considered natural.

The point of this example isn't whether or not same-sex marriage is good or bad. People sometimes have strong beliefs one way or the other. The example is given to illustrate the point that claiming something to be natural or unnatural does nothing to move the discussion forward. Arguing that certain social norms are natural or unnatural is weak and fallacious because it says nothing about whether or not that action is good or bad. Society used to think of marriages between two different races as unnatural, but we recognize that as foolish reasoning today. Highlighting these historical shifts in society's understanding of what is "natural" can demonstrate the potential toxic bigotry involved with using the faulty logic of an appeal to the natural and unnatural as the thing that determines whether something is good or bad.

Pointing out logical fallacies or flaws in your opponent's argument might cause them to hold their beliefs more strongly and double down on their fallacious reasoning.

That is why during the discussion of various ideas and principles, it is important to simply explain the potential dangers of accepting a fallacious form of logic and not mock them for appealing to nature.

Once you've learned to detect the fallacious use of the appeal to nature, learn to present it to your opponent in a calm way. Don't waste an opportunity to point out a flaw in their argument by jumping on the fallacy and saying, "Ah! Got you! That's a fallacy!" That's a big no. You will only enlarge the divide between you and your opponent and make it difficult to continue a reasonable discussion. Recognizing fallacy in a discussion will help with your own inner dialogue as you come to understand complex ideas using strong reason.

The use of the appeal to nature usually consists of the following three parts:

- Person A states their position X.
- Person A claims that X is natural.
- X is therefore asserted as good.

An Example with Ethan and Emily

Ethan and Emily were hanging out at the park when they saw Carlos sitting on a bench. They hadn't seen him for a few days, so Ethan and Emily jogged over to see how he was doing.

"Hey, Carlos! What's up? Why are you not playing today?" Ethan eagerly asked him.

"I haven't been feeling well these past few days," Carlos

explained. "I thought it would be a good idea to come to the park for some fresh air," he continued.

"Have you been to the doctor lately?" Emily asked with a curious look.

Carlos explained, "Yeah, and the doctor told me to take some medication, but my parents are on this all-natural remedy cure they want me to try." He gave a rough sounding cough and continued, "My parents are wary of things prescribed by the doctor."

Ethan and Emily both thought this seemed odd. If Carlos wasn't getting better maybe he should consider taking the medication the doctor had prescribed.

Ethan replied to Carlos with curiosity, "Have your parents considered that since you are not getting better that maybe they should consider using the medication prescribed by the doctor?"

"Yeah, I've asked them about doing that," he said between coughs, "but they are worried about the chemicals that are in the medication that was prescribed." Carlos weakly shrugged his shoulders.

The twins were called back, leaving them alone with their thoughts to consider what had just happened.

What Happened?

It's important to note that in this dialogue Carlos wasn't the one being fallacious in his reasoning. He was going along with what his parents had told him to do. On the other hand, Carlos's parents were operating under an appeal to nature: he should take natural remedies instead of the medication prescribed by his doctor, because the doctor-prescribed medication is unnatural.

The dialogue starts with Carlos making the claim on behalf of his parents that because the natural remedies are natural, they are, therefore, better. Then when Ethan and Emily pointed out that maybe Carlos should consider the doctor prescribed medication, he flipped the argument the other way by pointing out that the doctor-prescribed medication is bad because it's unnatural. The fallacy assumes natural is good and unnatural is bad, without ever acknowledging the argument being brought forward.

Carlos did not address any point being made by Ethan or Emily. He simply put forward his statements and assumed they were logically sound.

For another example, imagine you are at your annual family reunion. You decide to spice up some of the discussion when one of your environmentally-minded relatives brings up the importance of protecting our ecosystem with clean energy.

You decide to provide a rebuttal (calmly) that we should continue allowing the use of fossil fuels because it provides cheap energy that helps increase economic prosperity. Your Aunt Rebecca responds by saying that we should not interfere because it disrupts the natural state of the ecosystem. As it has been shown previously with jasmine berries, natural isn't always good. If your aunt were to acknowledge the point about the berries, she would be admitting that naturalness isn't always good.

Your aunt failed to address your point by just implying that maintaining the ecosystem's natural state is always best. Instead of falling into a lazy argument tactic, she should have brought up points on how fossil fuels could negatively affect our ecosystem in a way that brings harm to us, while clean energy does not. Whether or not you agree with those points isn't the important takeaway. It's that we need to clearly articulate the actual reasons we are offering for our argument being sound, not just rely on an appeal to nature as the proof itself.

Tuttle Twins Takeaway

Fight this fallacy by first learning to identify the use of an appeal to nature. You can do this by recognizing that when people simply use nature to support a conclusion, it adds nothing of substance in the discussion of ideas and principles. Next, remember the two basic flaws to point out within the argument. Natural isn't only hard to define but societal standards for natural change over time. Also, natural doesn't necessarily mean good.

ANECDOTAL

Generalizations can help us make sense of the world, but limited experience and isolated examples shouldn't replace a solid argument or actual evidence.

The most dangerous thing about living by the ocean is shark attacks.

I know because my cousin was bitten while surfing last year.

True, people of color are being sentenced more harshly.

But the judge goes to my church, and he doesn't seem racist.

A Story is Not Proof

When debating a friend, you have to think quickly, and it may be tempting to use personal stories about yourself, a relative, or someone you heard about as valid evidence. Oftentimes using these personal stories as evidence commits a common logical mistake, the *anecdotal fallacy*.

The anecdotal fallacy occurs when a person draws a conclusion about the causation of some event based upon anecdotal evidence. Anecdotal evidence is based solely on the personal experience of one person or a small number of people. Although these personal stories may be compelling, they cannot be used as blanket statements to establish facts for the general population. Here are a couple of examples of the fallacy in action:

Flying is a very dangerous way to travel. I know this because my aunt was in a plane crash. We will be much safer if we drive.

Scientists and researchers say smoking causes you to die young. But my grandma Laberta smoked like a chimney and lived until she was 90! So clearly the scientists are wrong.

Both of these examples use personal stories that are outside of the statistical norm; flying is safer than driving and smoking increases your chances of dying young. By using anecdotal examples like a single plane crash, you create an emotionally charged, but poorly reasoned, argument. These stories do nothing to address the researched statistics of large populations because one example isn't enough evidence to disprove the norm.

The anecdotal fallacy can be tempting for creating emotional appeal for your argument. Stories have a great psychological influence over us. The media knows this. They often opt to report more heavily on stories that garner highly emotional responses. Media outlets would much rather report on a fatal plane crash than a car accident involving injured drivers. Why? Because they want to attract as many viewers and readers as possible and the most shocking stories draw people in.

There's a saying for news media: "when a dog bites a man, that is not news, but when a man bites a dog, that is news." Of course, car crashes (or dog bites) are much more common than plane crashes (or human bites). Yet, a plane crash adds more shock value, making us more likely to watch their reports from the crash site. You must remember the amount of shock a story packs in does nothing to increase the probability of that type of event recurring.

In addition, those shocking stories fail to strengthen your argument. The goal should be to address the other person's argument with strong reasoning. You should not try to earn shock value by thinking of a personal story to counter your opponent's position because it does nothing to undermine their argument.

You must resist the temptation to earn emotional points from your opponent or the audience. Even if the story sways the position of your opponent or audience, it has done nothing towards developing knowledge for you, your opponent, or those listening. Personal and anecdotal stories distort facts and muddy the understanding of truth.

Because the news continuously commits this fallacy, some people have become disproportionately fearful of unlikely events, such as terrorism, kidnapping, and shark attacks. This blurring of facts can have potentially dangerous real world implications. This is why discussing facts is important in debating. The spread of misinformation can be toxic and dangerous. It is so important to learn and recognize when this fallacious argument tactic is being used, either by yourself or others. This will lead to more thoughtful discussion, a better understanding of ideas, and the discovery of reliable truth.

The use of the anecdotal argument usually is formed when:

- Person A said X happened once when Y happened.

- Person A concludes X happens every time Y happens.

An Example with Ethan and Emily

Ricky walked into the hallway where Ethan, Emily, and Jane were talking. He had a huge smile on his face.

"What happened to you?" Emily asked.

Ricky flexed his arm muscle. "I'm going to start hitting the gym. I've finally realized the answer to making the starting squad this season and now I'm sure I'll make it!"

Ethan cocked an eyebrow. "What? How do you figure that?"

Ricky explained, "Marcus has been going to the gym for over a year now, and he started the whole second half of the season last year. It's a cinch!"

Jane frowned, looking at Ricky, "Don't you think there's more to Marcus starting than just hitting the gym a couple months before the season?"

Ethan thought of the season that just ended. "Ricky, I don't remember your making it to any extra practices last year."

Ricky shook his head. "Anyway, Jason joined the gym two months ago, and he got a recruitment letter from State U. this week!"

Ricky bolted down the hall, fist-pumping the air, leaving Ethan and Emily to wonder what happened.

What Happened?

Ricky made an anecdotally fallacious argument.

He used two stories, one about Marcus and another about Jason, to support his belief that working out at the gym would assure him of athletic success.

He failed to take into account many other factors that could have led to success for Marcus and Jason. Marcus might be naturally more athletically talented than most of the other team members. Or, it may be the case that most of Marcus's success comes from his participation in extra team practices. Likewise, Jason working out at the gym two months ago had little effect on why the State U has sent him a recruitment letter.

Extraordinary claims require extraordinary proof, not particular parts of a story of what happened to a friend.

Ricky's desired outcome is so strong in his mind that he has rationalized a chain of causation from working out—also just being at the gym—to the success he desires.

Jane points out an important flaw in Ricky's reasoning.

Much like in the examples mentioned earlier, Ricky is only considering his chosen evidence. With the anecdotal fallacy, this is often the use of a personal story, but for Ricky, this is choosing part of the story as reasoning for Marcus' success with the team. Ricky fails to account for the other factors (evidence) of Marcus's success—natural athleticism, attending practice, running, and more.

Essentially, Ricky is picking an anecdotal piece of the evidence to determine his reasoning for going to the gym.

For example, if someone in a car accident wasn't wearing her seatbelt and didn't get injured, does that support an argument that seat belts are not necessary, or are even counter-productive? No; all anecdotal evidence needs to be backed up with data.

For example, instead of just using statistics in your argument, you could use anecdotal evidence to support this point, such as naming circumstances where a seat belt saved the life of a friend of yours in a car accident. In this case you're not being fallacious because you provided your fact-based reasoning with additional anecdotes to support that reasoning. That's not being fallacious; that's just good argumentation.

Anecdotes can be analogies *illustrating* proof, but are not, themselves, proof of anything.

Tuttle Twins Takeaway

Avoid anecdotal fallacies by focusing on *real* evidence, not stories about a single person or a small group. Be especially careful when the single person in question is you. Avoiding this fallacy will strengthen your thinking about the real world, but it does not mean that you must, or should, avoid anecdotes completely. Remain a skeptical thinker and evaluate anecdotes according to the actual value they provide. It does not matter whether an anecdote is wrong. The anecdote may very well be perfectly true in that instance. But, what might be correct in one case is not necessarily correct in all other cases.

The
SHARPSHOOTER

Our brains have a tendency to look for patterns in information, but patterns are often only a coincidence. We have to be careful not to draw conclusions that aren't true.

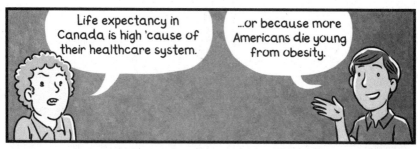

Life expectancy in Canada is high 'cause of their healthcare system.

...or because more Americans die young from obesity.

FDR's New Deal and WWII ended the Great Depression.

Looking at all factors, economic growth came after the war ended and FDR died.

By these numbers, this law saved a hundred tigers last year.

But it incentivized poaching, which killed **thousands**.

Sharpshooting Fallaciously

Imagine this scenario: When walking your dog one afternoon, you hear gunshots down the road by the neighbor's old barn. You decide to run over and investigate. As you walk up, you see a man holding dual pistols and dressed up like he's from the wild west. As you get closer, the gunslinger walks over to the barn he was shooting at and paints a target with a bullseye around some bullet holes in the barn.

The gunslinger turns around, sees you, and begins pointing out all of the bullseyes of the targets he has just hit. What a shot right? The gunslinger claims to be a sharpshooter after painting targets around where he initially shot. See the problem?

Enter the temptation of the *sharpshooter*. Cause and effect have been reversed. The (fake) sharpshooter cherry-picked the placement of the targets to where he landed his shots.

To demonstrate this in a debate situation, imagine the shots that were fired by the gunslinger as the random data points collected. Some of those data points come in clusters. If you or your opponent only choose the clusters that support your point, you are behaving like the sharpshooter.

Consider the claim that *men are more likely to die in the workplace than women*. From this, your friend Samuel claims that society is only focusing on and concerned with women's protections in the workplace.

The problem, of course, is that Samuel avoided other data that proves his argument wrong, such as the fact that men are more likely to participate in more dangerous, labor-intensive jobs. This fact disproves Samuel's theory that concerns about women's safety are the reason why men are more likely to die at work, but he ignored this information to make his own case.

You should always have all the important facts and information on the table to make sure you best support your claim. To avoid wasting your opponent's time and your time, you will want to put proper research and thought into your argument to avoid engaging in confirmation bias (looking for facts to affirm your prior beliefs). The internet is the perfect landscape to kindle confirmation bias, as it allows people to locate websites that will fit their narrative. To be a skilled debater, you will want to have as much information supporting your ideas as possible. Engaging in confirmation bias and using the sharpshooter's tactics will not get you to this goal.

The sharpshooter typically happens when:

- Person A is presented with multiple data points.

- Person A chooses data point C to fit claim X and ignores the other data points.

An Example with Ethan and Emily

Ethan and Emily were at church on Sunday with their parents when they noticed the church choir was accepting more singers. Their parents wanted them to join up to be more involved with the church community, so Ethan and Emily decided to talk to the choir director. This is when they ran into their friend Dasha.

As Ethan and Emily looked at the list, Emily noticed something. She looked over at Ethan and asked, "Why are more girls signed up than boys?"

Ethan contemplated this for a second, then responded, "I don't know really. I'm not exactly excited to be in the choir, though, so maybe boys just don't like it as much."

Ethan began writing his name on the list and he noticed that their friend Dasha was standing behind them, presumably waiting to sign up for the church choir as well.

"I overheard you two discussing the list and how you noticed more girls are signed up than boys," she said to the twins with her arms crossed. "More girls sign up than boys because girls are just better at singing," she proclaimed.

"Hmm. Maybe they are, but I don't know if this church list can prove that," Ethan responded to Dasha with a questioning tone.

"Well, the list is right here, and there must be a reason more girls sign up than boys," she asserted as she wrote her name on the list.

After writing her name on the list, she left the twins wondering what just happened.

What Happened?

Dasha likely believed girls are better singers than boys before she used the list of choir members as evidence to support her claim. She is cherry-picking data, just like the sharpshooter who drew his target around his bullet holes after firing his gun.

This is fallacious reasoning, because it avoids taking into account all sorts of other data: the fact that more girls sign up provides no evidence about a person's singing ability; it doesn't take into account other church choirs' boy-to-girl ratio; it fails to consider personal preference and doesn't even include random chance. The point is, Dasha was seizing an opportunity to use information that fit her claim.

This isn't to say that you must account for every single data point and alternative explanation imaginable. Using data is oftentimes crucial in providing a well-reasoned argument, and using data to support your claim is not fallacious. The key is to not ignore data that doesn't fit your claim or warp circumstantial data to fit your claim.

Scientific research might be the area that most commonly commits this fallacy. For example, a scientist wants to research a hypothesis or, to use a term consistent with the other fallacies we've discussed, they are looking to make a claim.

When scientists collect data, they're supposed to have a hypothesis in mind and analyze whether the data fit their hypothesis. In this scenario, after gathering the data, they find that their claim or hypothesis was proven wrong. But imagine if the researcher was not willing to admit defeat. The temptation might be very strong to only pick out the data that fits their claim and omit the counter evidence from their research. When the researcher presents the research, they will be committing the Texas sharpshooter fallacy because they chose to cherry-pick data that fits their narrative. Scientific evidence must be repeatable by other researchers.

Tuttle Twins Takeaway

A major takeaway for this fallacy is to make sure you avoid confirmation bias. When discussing ideas, you want all the vital information on the table, including information that's counter to your argument. That means information that might provide evidence that's counter to your argument. If you want to grasp ideas and gain knowledge, you must learn to avoid becoming the Texas sharpshooter.

MIDDLE GROUND

When two extremes are each claimed to be true, a person will sometimes argue that a compromise position somewhere between the two must be the actual truth.

Hey, Sue. Look. That's a golden eagle!

No, Richard. It's just a big turkey vulture.

Then can we just agree that it's a California condor?

At a genetic level there are only two genders: male and female.

Many people don't feel that they fit the mold of society's gender norms.

I respect that, so let's decide that there are unlimited genders.

Man in the Middle

When you're presented with two strong arguments from two friends on completely opposite sides of an issue, it may be difficult to address the quality of both. The separate arguments or positions will require research and thought to properly address them.

The problem is, when you're in a conversation or argument, you don't have much time to analyze the positions. You must think quickly to determine your position. Is one argument better than the other? Are both wrong? Or is the solution somewhere in the middle? This can be hard to determine in the heat of the moment, which leads toward a temptation to compromise, sometimes unnecessarily.

This temptation is known as the *middle ground fallacy*. Imagine you and your friend Mario have opposing viewpoints about the color of the sky. Mario says the sky is red but you say the sky is blue. Mario is convinced he's right because he's researched and thought about his position. (He must have forgotten to look up.)

Now imagine a yardstick. In your mind, place your opinion on one side of the yardstick and Mario's opinion on the other. Hold that image in your head. This is the spectrum of opinions between you and Mario that will be useful in explaining the problem with the middle ground later.

After some back and forth, Mario realizes you both hold extremes on a spectrum of opinions, and there must be a balanced point of view. To compromise between the two positions, he says the sky is purple. This claim is accepting partial truth from both extremes, and you decide to accept it.

The problem is, of course, that the sky *is* blue. Mario has not addressed whether the sky is actually blue or not; he assumed the two extremes must be false and the middle ground true. He assumed that based on your established spectrum of ideas for the color of the sky that the answer must be somewhere in the middle of the spectrum. It may feel good to find a compromise or common ground of agreement, but your position on the color of the sky has not been proven, and neither has Mario's, based on the conclusion that the sky is purple.

If anything, you've not only weakened your argument, but provided strength to Mario's argument. Instead of holding your ground on the position and principle you know to be true, you compromised, which gave legitimacy to Mario's argument when none was due. The use of the middle ground fallacy leaves both sides with a partial emotional victory.

Imagine a similar situation, with some higher stakes and real world implications: Mario thinks slavery is good and you think slavery is always bad. You look to Amy to find a compromise (middle ground) between the two sides of the spectrum. In this situation she is of the mindset that when presented with two extremes, the answer must lie in between the two positions, and concludes that slavery is sometimes legitimate.

In an argument with such high stakes, it's vitally important to address your opponent's argument head on. Don't give in to temptations of appeasing your opponent by providing legitimacy with a compromise when absolutely none is due.

The use of a middle ground fallacy usually consists of the

following three parts:

- Position A and C are two extreme positions.

- B is a position that rests in the middle of A and C.

- Therefore B is claimed to be the correct position.

An Example with Ethan and Emily

"What game should we play today?" Emily curiously asked Ethan after arriving at the park.

Ethan thought for a second and decided, "We should play some volleyball. The park has nets and a ball. I rarely see anyone our age try to play."

Emily contemplated this, then replied, "Well, that sounds fun, but I'd rather shoot some hoops like when we were younger."

"We haven't played volleyball in ages, though," Ethan replied. "How about this? We'll ask Dexter to play and see what he wants to do," Ethan suggested.

Emily agreed and they walked over to Dexter to see which game he wanted to play.

After asking Dexter, he replied, "Well, I don't really want to play either of them."

Ethan curiously asked, "And why is that?"

"Well, I want to focus on the sports that are popular here. You know, football and baseball, because they are worth practicing for school and could lead to going pro someday!" Dexter explained.

"Maybe we should meet in the middle of these options and come up with our own game instead. It's probably the best option," Dexter said.

Ethan and Emily reluctantly agreed but later questioned Dexter's reasoning and wondered what happened.

What Happened?

Dexter assumed a new game was the middle option, falling to the middle ground fallacy. Although it was a short dialogue, Dexter seemed to assume that both Ethan and Emily's choices were a waste of time.

Imagining our handy yardstick again, Dexter was placing volleyball on one side of the stick and basketball on the other. Seeing these two options as extremes neither could agree on, he assumed a new game was the middle ground answer. He assumed that Ethan and Emily's choices were extremes because of their disagreement. Thus, he found the middle ground to be the only option.

Dexter never tried to resolve Ethan and Emily's dilemma of what to play; he immediately took the middle ground as the only option. This is a common example of the middle ground fallacy, often seen in political discourse.

For example, imagine you're at a family event where all the aunts and uncles gather together. You have various Republicans and Democrats among your aunts and uncles, who inevitably begin to debate politics. The argument devolves into a typical, mundane back and forth about the common disagreements between the two sides. You politely interject by mentioning the possibility that both Republicans and

Democrats have it wrong, and instead maybe libertarians and socialists have some insight to provide.

One of your uncles disagrees, saying that both of those alternative viewpoints are far too extreme for consideration. Your uncle takes a step further, claiming Republicans and Democrats hold proper positions because those are the established middle ground positions along our political spectrum.

Your uncle is, of course, assuming that the middle of the spectrum holds the answers. He goes on to claim that libertarians want full-on anarchy: allowing anyone in the country, legalizing everything, and fighting against almost all government authority. His claim for socialists is that they want the corrupt government to control everything, increase welfare, and increase taxes way too high. He concludes by claiming these extreme ideas would be more accepted if they were actually plausible or reasonable, and reiterating that the answer is only found in the middle.

Your uncle's position in this situation is an example of the Overton window, a term used to explain the concept that only certain political ideas are seen as reasonable and politically possible—a window of appealing options to choose from, where those that fall outside the window are not appealing or considered too controversial.

This Overton window of ideas is a form of the middle ground fallacy. Your point wasn't that libertarians or socialist are always completely correct, or even that those positions should absolutely be the accepted viewpoints. You were merely pointing out that those ideas should be heard and properly represented, because the answer might not be within the Overton window of political ideas. Limiting ideas during a discussion is a missed opportunity for thoughtful discussion.

Tuttle Twins Takeaway

Fight the middle ground fallacy by focusing on the ideas and arguments being presented to you, not taking the easy way through compromise. You learn and progress by seeking the truth in a debate. By addressing the ideas all along the spectrum, you are not only more apt to find the answer but avoid giving legitimacy to arguments that haven't done the work of providing solid reasoning. Doing so will help strengthen your ideas and arguments.

TU QUOQUE
Latin for "You Also"

When a person is wrong or being hypocritical, they should avoid the temptation to shift the criticism back to the person making the point. Instead, consider the merits of their argument.

You, Too!

Sometimes a fallacy might sneak up on you like an instinct, one which you cannot help but use to attack your opponent. This chapter's fallacy is one that you've probably used or has been used on you multiple times.

Imagine the following scenario: Betsy has just started a new job at a local restaurant in town. After a few training shifts, she starts to get the hang of things. After a night shift, she begins to spot sweep the floor, but she only sweeps the parts of the floor with visible debris. A coworker sees what she's doing and stops her in her tracks.

"Whoa, whoa, whoa. You can't sweep like that. You have to sweep the entire floor, or you'll miss a spot and end up with only a partially clean floor," he says.

Confused, she responds, "But I've seen you do it like this multiple times!"

The problem with this response is that she's dismissed her coworker's claim simply because she sees it as hypocritical. Instead of focusing on why her coworker doesn't want her to improperly sweep the floor, the "Well, you did it, too" response focuses on the hypocrisy committed by her coworker. Simply put, by committing this fallacy she has fallaciously dismissed her opponent's argument because she thinks the speaker is a hypocrite.

The fallacy presented above is called the *tu quoque*. This fallacy is closely related to the ad hominem fallacy covered in previous chapters. As you have been able to detect, the tu quoque fallacy is an attack on you or your opponent's personal character, like the ad hominem fallacy. However, the tu quoque is when you specifically call out the hypocrisy of the person making the argument. Understanding this variation of the fallacy is necessary to help you better respond to its use. It's bad reasoning to assume an argument is wrong just because the person making the argument acted inconsistently.

Address this fallacy by avoiding the pointing of fingers—the "Well, you do it" tactic of the fallacy. Instead, simply further the discussion by asking why they act inconsistently. Asking a question about your opponent's claim is a much more peaceful method of debate, plus you avoid making a fallacious assertion.

By asking a question about your opponent's actions, you should receive further clarification and further reasoning for their claim. However, you should not stop there because you still need to make a claim of your own to refute your opponent. By avoiding pointing fingers, you stand a better chance of earning points from your opponent and the crowd. You should never make claims of hypocrisy!

The tu quoque fallacy usually comes with three main parts:

- Person A makes claim X.

- Person B claims that Person A's past actions or claims are inconsistent with claim X.

- Person B concludes: Therefore X is false.

An Example with Ethan and Emily

Ethan and Emily decided to go to the movies on a cold and rainy Saturday with their friend Lexi. After standing in the concession stand line, it was their turn to put in their order.

"Hmm, I would like a large popcorn with a small soda," Ethan told the worker at the register.

"I would like the same thing, please," Lexi said to the worker after Ethan.

"Emily, what would you like?" Ethan kindly asked Emily as she waited in line.

"I'll just have a popcorn and water, please," she said to the worker.

The three waited at the end of the counter for their order to be completed.

Emily decided to break the silence as they stood waiting for their food and drinks, saying, "You know, you shouldn't drink soda. It's bad for your health!"

"I know, I know, but I still enjoy it as a special treat when we go to the movies," Ethan explained as he nodded his head.

Lexi was thinking to herself as Ethan responded, then said to Emily, "Wait, I saw you drink soda yesterday when we were hanging out. So what do you know if you don't even take your own advice?"

Emily just shrugged it off as they walked into the movie;

however, Ethan and Emily had an opportunity to gather their thoughts and discuss what had happened.

What Happened?

This situation holds a lot of similarities to our janitorial example from before. Emily observed that Ethan and Lexi had just made an unhealthy decision in their beverage of choice for the movie. After Emily made this observation, she decided to give her opinion on how soda is unhealthy for you.

Ethan had a reasonable response to Emily's judgement of soda being unhealthy—that he chooses to drink only on special occasions (like going to the movies). Lexi decided to come back with a snarkier comment, the "you did it, too." It was mentioned earlier that tu quoque is related to the ad hominem fallacy because Lexi's claim to counter Emily is simply a critique on Emily's character.

Lexi's claim is focusing on the previous actions or history of Emily instead of focusing on Emily's actual claim. Like the ad hominem fallacy, tu quoque is an argument based on the person making the argument instead of the argument itself.

Lexi wasn't addressing the health problem Emily was raising. She was providing a reaction to Emily making the claim as her argument.

Imagine this real world example: You are with your Uncle Joe on a family camping trip and you start talking politics.

As you continue the conversation, you start discussing

the importance of free markets in developing economic growth, so you go on to claim that the United States should implement economic policies like Hong Kong, because they take their free market principles more seriously!

Of course, Uncle Joe being Uncle Joe, he takes issue with your claim. He comes back by saying, "If you like Hong Kong so much, why don't you live there?"

For one, you didn't say everyone should pack up their things and move to Hong Kong because it's a paradise. You presented a claim that involved more than just Hong Kong: that free markets are good for the economy and Hong Kong is an example of this policy going well. You were implying that the United States should learn from those policies, not that everyone should move there. But more importantly, your moving or not moving to Hong Kong does nothing to address your argument.

You need to learn this format of the fallacy that was just demonstrated. This example uses a less obvious and possibly worse use of hypocrisy. For example, it's plausible that Emily had drunk soda the day before. This would make her a hypocrite, but this still doesn't address her argument.

In your Uncle Joe's example, his rebuttal doesn't attack your claim, nor does it actually point out hypocrisy. It attempts to, but it doesn't take into account the likelihood that you've lived in the U.S. for a long time, plus have various reasons for staying, for example because your family and friends are here. These personal attacks don't feel good, so remember to not use them on others!

Tuttle Twins Takeaway

Fight this fallacy by remembering to focus on your opponent's *argument*. This means you must learn to recognize the fallacy to avoid its use and learn to address it when it's used on you. That's the best way to keep the focus on the ideas of an argument. So remember that just because someone doesn't follow the claims they're preaching doesn't mean what they're preaching is wrong. Peacefully pointing this out can go a long way in furthering your discussion of ideas!

The
FALLACY
FALLACY

Pointing out a fallacy of logic is great, but don't assume the debate is won. One mistake doesn't necessarily discredit the entire argument.

Did you just say this is a "Slippery Slope" to a life of unhealthy behaviors?

Your fallacious argument is the only problem I see. I can stop at anytime.

Yeah, I know most sheeple believe the Earth is spherical. That's the Bandwagon fallacy!

More evidence that the Earth is flat!

That's So Meta...

As you learn more about logic and reasoning, you will face opponents with varying debate skill levels. Some will take pride in not only creating a thoughtful conversation, but also in their ability to properly argue for their claims. These more skillful opponents will make mistakes; it's part of learning to properly argue. But sometimes your skillful opponent will get too caught up on the reasoning behind your claims, making them susceptible to the *fallacy fallacy*.

The fallacy fallacy is when your opponent claims your argument contains a logical fallacy, so your claim must be false. To help understand this fallacy, remember to focus on a person's conclusions during an argument or debate; you must not get caught up on your opponent using a fallacy.

The point in recognizing fallacies is to help pinpoint problems within an argument and the reasons someone comes to a conclusion, especially if it's a bad conclusion. To help keep the argument on track, think about what the conclusion says and if you think you agree or disagree. Then move on to the reasoning. But remember, you have to provide a strong reasoned-based response against their claim whether they've used a fallacy or not.

Your position or objection to your opponent's conclusion is not strengthened by simply pointing out your opponent's use of a fallacy. All you've done is point out a fallacy, not validated or invalidated a claim. However, it does help progress the conversation forward.

There's also a good chance someone can provide a mostly solid argument that hits multiple good points but they add one fallaciously. If you were to dismiss the person's conclusion merely because of one use of a fallacy, you would not only be committing the fallacy fallacy, but this doesn't actually address the important aspect of their argument, the claim.

If the claim is good and the reasoning is *mostly* good, it might be best to focus on that to help further thoughtful and productive discussion. Just because your opponent fails to completely prove their position, doesn't make them or their claim wrong.

Unnecessarily pointing out fallacies as reasons to dismiss someone's argument is not only a waste of time but limits your intake of alternative ideas and viewpoints. Sometimes people have great ideas but are just bad at reasoning.

Using the fallacy fallacy is a dishonest tactic used to convince your opponent or the crowd that you've "won" the argument. However, using this fallacious tactic does very little, if anything, to address the claims being made. It acts as a distraction to the important *ideas* that should be the focus. Understanding this fallacy is an important reminder that opponents who understand logical fallacies and want to "win" every conversation will be seeking any logical fallacy you use in order to dismiss your argument. Your opponent might use a phrase such as, *they are just being lazy and using an appeal to popularity.*

This is done in hopes of making the crowd more skeptical of your claims so they are more apt to accept your opponent's claim. Imagine the frustration you would feel!

Remember this before not only using fallacies but using the fallacy fallacy as well.

The fallacy fallacy comes with three main parts:

- Person A argues for position X that supports conclusion Z.

- Person B points out Person A's argument for Z contains a logical fallacy.

- Person B concludes conclusion Z *must* be false.

An Example with Ethan and Emily

Ethan and Emily were driving with their friend Deven on their way to the movies when the topic of healthy eating came up.

"Guys, guys! I've been doing this new meal plan and weight lifting to get in shape for football season," Deven excitedly said to Ethan and Emily.

Ethan responded by asking curiously, "Nice! What's the plan you have been doing?"

Deven leaned up between the two front seats, replying, "I can have a fast food burger every day if I want, or drink or eat just about everything." He continued, "See, the key is getting in your macronutrients, but when it comes down to it: food is food."

Emily responded with a feeling of suspicion, "So, you could have fast food every single day and then do a lifting routine, and be ready to go for football season?"

"Yes! Calories in, calories out! It's basic science and nutrition, guys," Deven replied as he leaned back in his seat.

Ethan turned to the back seat to face Deven. "Yeah, but wouldn't following those macronutrients with some fruits and vegetables be better? You know, some natural foods?"

"Hold up. You just committed a logical fallacy because you think just because fruits and vegetables are natural they must be good," Deven said as he waved his hand. "I'm in the middle of this great book on logical fallacies. It talks about how it's bad argumentation and a fallacy to assume something is good just because it's natural, so I'm going to stick with my meal plan," he continued.

The discussion ended as they arrived at the theater. But upon arriving home later, Ethan and Emily wondered what happened.

What Happened?

Ethan made the conclusion that Deven should eat something besides just fast food for his meal plan—that he should eat some fruits and vegetables. Deven quickly pushed Ethan's conclusion aside by pointing out the poorly reasoned conclusion Ethan made. But does this prove his conclusion wrong?

No. Deven has only proved that Ethan used some poor reasoning skills to try and prove his conclusion. There are many reasons to include various fruits and vegetables into your diet. Just because someone provides poor reasoning for why you should do so doesn't change the truth of the benefits of eating fruits and vegetables.

For example, imagine if Ethan didn't use the fallacy of appealing to nature to make his point. Instead, Ethan decides to claim that you should eat fruits and vegetables because it will make you fly.

Of course this claim is ridiculous because you know that fruits and vegetables don't make you fly. This would quickly become common knowledge if it were true!

If you choose to eat fruits and vegetables because someone convinces you they will make you fly, that doesn't prove that fruits and vegetables are good or bad for you, just that you have bad reasoning skills. Remember, people are sometimes correct by accident!

You will likely encounter this same fallacious reasoning during real world conversations and debates. For example, imagine making the claim that we should consider how new business regulations often hurt small business owners more than big corporations by stifling innovation and propping up failing corporations.

But instead of using this line of reasoning for why we should decrease regulations, you say that people who oppose deregulation on business are just too stupid to understand basic economics! Does this alternative faulty line of reasoning change whether it's correct that we should or should not deregulate businesses? No. It's just that one line of reasoning is better than others. Also, remember the point is to keep your opponent's mind open to new ideas.

Tuttle Twins Takeaway

Remember to keep your conversations on the *concepts* and *ideas* moving forward. Don't get caught up on whether or not your opponent's line of reasoning is fallacious. Instead focus on the concepts or ideas being presented in the claim. You should still point out when your opponent uses fallacious tactics, but get the conversation back to the discussion topic as quickly as possible. Remember that it's not about winning the debate at all cost, so avoid using logical fallacies to prove your point or disprove your opponent's claim. It's about being open to learning about and understanding new ideas.

So that's it! You now have all kinds of knowledge about how to think more clearly and argue your points better than ever. They don't teach this stuff in school... Could you imagine all the students pointing out the logical fallacies their teacher keeps using?

The world is a confusing place full of people spouting wrong ideas and using bad data to advance their agenda or simply prove themselves right.

It's up to us to sort through that mess and find what's true.

We hope the information in this guide is helpful. It has certainly been helpful for us to learn about.

Like many guidebooks, this book is meant to be more of a reference than a book you read in one sitting. (But if you managed to do that, big kudos to you!) You'll want to peruse it here and there in the months and years to come—especially if you notice someone using one of these fallacies and you want to brush up on it a bit so you can better explain why their argument is incorrect.

With great knowledge of logical fallacies comes... yep, great responsibility! So use this information wisely.

—The Tuttle Twins